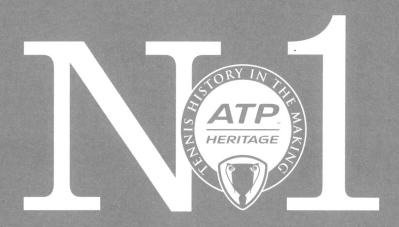

Nº1

CELEBRATING **40 YEARS** OF
THE ULTIMATE ACHIEVEMENT

A rare achievement only attained by the legendary champions of our sport.

A year-long journey, played at 65 tournaments across 31 countries against an army of supremely talented and uncompromising opponents.

A brutal test of athleticism, technique, physical endurance and mental strength.

A quest to find the motivation to push harder after victory, to rise above heart-breaking loss, to continue the relentless pursuit to the peak of world tennis.

To stand at year-end, alone and victorious as the **ATP World Tour No. 1.**

Brad Drewett describes what it takes to become a year-end ATP World Tour No.1.

Introduction

2013 marks a significant milestone for the ATP – a point in time at which we celebrate the 40th anniversary of the Emirates ATP Rankings.

First launched on August 23, 1973, the rankings have lain at the core of our sport over the past 40 years – a true measure of excellence and consistency, and a means through which greatness is ultimately defined in the game of men's professional tennis.

Over the past five decades, the landscape of men's professional tennis has changed radically as the sport has expanded to cover all corners of the globe. From the early dominance of players from the United States and Australia - traditional powerhouse nations of the pre-Open Era - men's professional tennis has become a truly global sport with nations as far and wide as Japan, Serbia, Uzbekistan, Latvia and Bulgaria all counting representatives among the higher echelons of the sport today.

As players from all nations battle to succeed on the ATP World Tour, the rankings have gradually taken on more and more significance, becoming the lifeblood of the Tour, an intrinsic part of the fabric of men's professional tennis. The rankings provide a barometer that judges all players equally and fairly, with no exceptions. Today, the ATP World Tour's truly global nature underlines the importance of a uniform world ranking system – a critical component of the Tour not only for our players, but also for our sport as a whole.

Scaling the summit of world tennis is without question one of the most brutal physical and mental tests in all sport – it means triumphing at the end of an 11-month battle, fought out across 65 tournaments and 31 countries, where only supreme strength combined with exquisite talent prevails. Only the strongest survive as one-on-one battles of gladiatorial proportions unfold before the eyes of the world throughout the year. And at the end of the season, only one man stands alone as the year-end ATP World Tour No. 1.

During the course of the past 40 years, only 16 players can lay claim to the ultimate prize of finishing the season as year-end No. 1. That remarkably low number says everything there is to say about the magnitude of this achievement.

The players featured in this book are part of an exclusive group to have achieved this feat. They are the true legends of our sport - those that have marked the history books; they are the pioneers whose legacies will live on to inspire future generations.

We hope you enjoy this unique publication marking the 40th anniversary of the Emirates ATP Rankings, honouring these great champions of our sport.

Brad Drewett

Brad Drewett
1958-2013

Contents

No. 1 - The Greatest Prize Of All

By Ed Smith

For 40 years, men's tennis has had an official No. 1. The accolade is now one of the most fiercely contested and highly prized titles in all sport.

Sports often invent new measures of greatness, and no one knows whether they will capture the public's imagination or not. Forty years ago, when tennis introduced the concept of a definitive '**World No. 1**', it was unclear whether the idea would become central to the sport. It has. Tennis fans have delighted in following the battles and rivalries of champion players as they try to scale the highest peak of them all. Quite simply, we all want to know who is the best in the world.

There are two standard ways of gauging a sport's ultimate champion. The first is via knock-out competition, historic stand-alone events such as Grand Slams, World Cups and Olympic finals. The second is through ranking systems, the relentless pursuit of excellence over the course of a whole year.

Until the 1970s, working out who was the world's best tennis player was a matter of judgment, perhaps even guesswork. Newspapers weighed in with tables, pundits proposed opinions. But there was no certain answer to the question, '**Who was the best player in the world this season?**' In contrast, there was never any doubt about who won the Grand Slams.

But the invention of a computerised ranking system in 1973 changed the balance of power. Suddenly, there was an objective measure of all-round excellence. Tennis fans could suddenly learn who was the best player, everything taken together, over the course of a whole season – in all conditions, on every surface, against every type of opponent.

No one could have predicted, however, how the ranking system would capture the public imagination. If we are honest, a points ranking system does not automatically have the same intrinsic romance as winning a Grand Slam.

A computer producing a number is not the same thing as an ecstatic crowd at Flushing Meadows cheering a champion as he raises the trophy. And a player can become World No. 1 at a relatively obscure event – as we learn in this book – or simply because his closest rival has lost a match.

But over time, the ranking system has become increasingly prestigious. Many players now consider being No. 1, especially year-end No. 1, as the true pinnacle. It has become one of the ultimate challenges in the sport. That shift in perception fits the reality of professional tennis: every match counts, there are no meaningless contests and, over time, the rankings reflect what the players deserve.

The rise of the ranking system has mirrored the remarkable evolution of tennis as a whole. Just as the ranking system occupies an exalted position inside tennis, tennis now enjoys a unique place in world sport. Over the 40 years since the rankings began, tennis has become

vastly more international. It is now truly a global sport. That has enhanced the power of the ranking system. Only a year-round ranking system could capture the challenge of playing on all surfaces, in almost every time-zone, across several continents. The growth in significance of the ranking system has reflected the way tennis has grown around the world.

Only 25 men have reached No. 1. And only 16 have achieved the status of year-end No. 1 The list tells its own story: from Nastase to Djokovic, via Borg and McEnroe, Sampras and Agassi, Federer and Nadal. Just reading the 16 names demonstrates that it is one of the most exclusive clubs in sport.

Tennis has enjoyed wonderful champions and thrilling rivalries at every stage of the last 40 years – never more so than right now. In fact, the status of the year-end rankings has benefitted from a vast stroke of luck: namely, the incredible quality of today's players and

the depth, complexity and sportsmanship that define their rivalries.

Over the last nine years, the No.1 spot has been shared by Roger Federer, Rafael Nadal and Novak Djokovic. Any sport would be lucky to have one player of such quality and charisma; tennis has three.

Each has raised the bar in a different way. Federer has combined the grace, elegance and sportsmanship of the perfect amateur alongside the astonishing consistency of the ultimate professional. Nadal's relentless pugilistic competitiveness, his fearless intensity on the court, is matched by exceptional modesty and courtesy. Djokovic knew he had to do something special to break into one of sport's greatest duopolies – the Federer-Nadal rivalry – to reach the top. The manner of his ascent to No.1, his phenomenal winning streak in 2011, proves the dizzying level of play required to get to the top of today's game.

No less remarkable was Federer's return to No.1 in 2012. It is here that we saw the rare significance of the rankings system. When he began his second assault on the top spot, Federer had already won 16 Grand Slams and was widely lauded as the greatest of all time. What more did he have to achieve, what could continue to motivate him? Watching Federer's form at the end of 2011 and then into 2012, you sensed how deeply he cared about regaining what had once been almost automatic: the right to be known, officially, as the world's best player.

That Djokovic had wrestled his way back to No.1 by the end of the Barclays ATP World Tour Finals in London proved the second rule of today's tennis: however hard it might be to reach No.1, however great the effort and resilience, only one thing is even harder: holding on to it.

With their contrasting styles and different personalities, the battle for supremacy at the top of men's tennis is one of the most absorbing narratives in world sport. And tennis fans know how fortunate we have been. When you are 1) amazed at the overall standard 2) find the protagonists thrillingly different and 3) don't know what's going to happen next – then you are one lucky sports fan. That is the state of men's tennis today. A true sporting golden age demands three things: exceptional quality, epic rivalries and dramatic uncertainty. Get the lot and the memories are indelible. Right now, men's tennis is hitting the ultimate sweet spot.

Consider exactly what goes in to becoming No.1, the breadth of qualities it demands. Today's champions must master three very different sporting challenges. First, they have to achieve exceptional levels of fitness and, just as important, improbable powers of recovery. In Melbourne in 2012, I watched Djokovic overcome Andy Murray over five brutal sets in the semi-final. Forty-eight hours later, he had to go through the same gruelling experience to beat Nadal in the final. That requires all-round fitness of the highest order. Not only does every No.1 have to run a lot of on-court miles, he has to move so fluidly that he avoids injury. It's a marathon that also demands balletic poise and balance.

Alongside the physical strain, tennis demands unique mental and psychological challenges. On a tennis court, you stand entirely alone, armed only with a racquet and your skills. Sitting on the chair between games, there is no team around you, no coach, no mentor. There is no hiding place, no way of taking a few moments out of the firing line, no private space to collect your thoughts or regain composure. Tennis players must be their own problem-solvers, self-reliant to the ultimate degree. Their face and body language is examined as minutely as their technique. On court, everything a tennis player does is public property. Keeping a clear mind and a cool head pushes even the most resilient competitors to the edge.

Finally, of course, tennis is a high skill sport demanding exceptional technical prowess. The best players command a dizzying array of shots in their offensive and defensive armoury. The technological and physiological evolution of tennis – the new strings and racquets, the stronger bodies – have not, after all, removed finesse from the game. Sure, the modern game demands power. But there is still remarkable artistry.

To reach the No. 1 spot, especially to become year-end No. 1, demands that the champion player masters tennis in all three of those dimensions: the physical, the mental and the technical. It is almost like having to combine the body of a triathlete, the mind of a chess master and the skill of a fine artist.

That is why, amid all this talk of the No. 1 tennis player, we should not lose sight of a wider battle for the top spot. There is a never-ending struggle for preeminence between sports as well as within them. All major sports continually

jostle for position, edging ahead, then falling behind their rivals.

In the 1920s, Babe Ruth made baseball the most loved sport in America, transforming the game with joyous hitting that fans rushed to watch. In the 1970s, boxing boasted four champions more than worthy of the heavyweight crown: Muhammad Ali, Joe Frazier, George Foreman and Ken Norton. Best of all, each boxer had deeply different styles, making the match-ups constantly unpredictable. Frazier and Norton pushed Ali to the limit, but both were annihilated by Foreman. So Foreman would certainly destroy Ali? No, he lost to Ali over eight rounds. The results were unpredictable, but the quality of the sport was always extraordinary.

Which sport, right now, can claim it is enjoying the most golden era, the purplest purple patch? A case could be made for football, led by the dazzling skills and flair of Spain and Barcelona. But I would argue that tennis leads world sport

today. The standard of play is breathtaking, the rivalries are complex, the narrative is dramatic and unpredictable.

I grew up a cricketer in a cricketing family. For most of my life, I never questioned the assumption that cricket was the greatest game in the world. But when I retired as a professional cricketer aged 31, I discovered a new freedom. No longer a practitioner, I was now simply a sports lover. And I watched sport with one criterion only: how much pleasure did it give me, how absorbing and moving did I find the experience? Tennis became my new sporting passion.

When we ask '**What is the hardest challenge in sport?**' the temptation is to jump to straight-forward endurance events such as the Tour de France. We naturally associate the epic suffering with grand achievement.

But becoming year-end No. 1 in tennis demands remarkable endurance, and yet

so much else besides. For a start, you have to compete across the whole year, around the world, never succumbing to fatigue or becoming jaded. And you will be tested in wildly different conditions, from a cool day on Centre Court at Wimbledon to a brutally humid afternoon in Shanghai. All the time, of course, you are playing for ranking points against the best in the world.

There is no easy path to No. 1, no short cut. It is a relentless examination of ability, willpower, endurance and skill. I know that many tennis insiders, who know far more about the sport than I do, believe that becoming year-end World No. 1 is the true pinnacle of tennis.

As an outsider, I might go one further. It might just be the pinnacle of world sport, full stop.

Year-End No. 1 Players

Throughout the 40-year history of the Emirates ATP Rankings, only 16 players can lay claim to the ultimate achievement of finishing the season as year-end No. 1. It is an exclusive group that comprises the greatest players in the history of the sport.

ATP™
WORLD TOUR
No.1
PRESENTED BY
Emirates

"I was No. 1, and whatever happens after that doesn't matter"

Ilie Nastase
1973

By Peter Bodo

It was only fitting that the ATP would end up celebrating the birth of the official year-end No.1 ranking with fireworks, even if they were of the human variety. Ilie Nastase, who became the first year-end No.1 in 1973, was one of the most colourful, explosive personalities the game has ever produced, as well as a harbinger of how much the game and players would change in what was still the relatively new Open Era. Nastase, a native of Bucharest,

Romania, emerged as a stunning natural talent at the age of 20, two years before the advent of Open tennis in 1968. He recorded his first wins over top international players (Tony Roche and Stan Smith) in 1967, and skyrocketed into the elite company of international icons like Rod Laver and Ken Rosewall when he won the coveted Italian Open title in 1970.

By then, the olive-skinned, long-haired hellion also had acquired the nickname that would trail

him for his entire career: **'Nasty.'** Although he became notorious for his gamesmanship, fear and loathing of officials, and outrageous – and frequently hilarious - emotional outbursts, he was also enormously charismatic. Nastase was an archetypal **'bad boy'** who also could charm a bird out of a tree, or bring a smile to the face of the most dour spectator.

When he was good, he was very, very good. When he was bad he was... **'Nasty.'**

'Before, the only rankings we had for the year-end No. 1 was completely a matter of opinion. Some different newspaper and magazine guys just doing rankings as they wanted and there was no **'official'** No. 1. It wasn't really fair. I was lucky that I played my best tennis in 1973, and that happened to be the year when the ATP rankings started."

Nastase was one of the most talented players ever to swing a racquet; he literally flowed across the court like liquid. No player has ever made it seem more like the racquet is a natural extension of his arm. But he was also high-strung and twitchy as a racehorse; any match he played could turn into an adventure, and not necessarily a pleasant one.

Nastase won two Grand Slam singles titles (US Open 1972, French Open 1973) and three in men's doubles; although he struggled to cope with the pressure at Grand Slam tournaments, he's one of just five players to win more than 100 titles across singles and doubles. He was at his best in the annual year-end Masters tournaments, which he won four times (1971, '72, '73 and '75).

Nastase didn't put much thought into becoming the first uncontested, ATP-endorsed year-end No. 1. For one thing, the rankings were a new gizmo, and nobody – including the players – knew how the new system would resonate. For another, during that first year of the computerised rankings, Nastase was busy cleaning up and winning almost everything in sight. Nastase won a staggering 14 tournaments in 1973, and hit the magical number on August 23rd, during the annual grass-court US Open tune-up tournament at the Orange Lawn Tennis Club in South Orange, New Jersey.

"It's funny, but I learned I was No. 1 on the same day that is Romania's Independence Day. But I wasn't able to celebrate because I was busy playing."

At the time, Nastase often fell back on the party line, claiming that he was focused solely on winning Grand Slam events rather than finishing the year as the top-ranked player. But now, he says: "Sure you want to win Grand Slams, but behind it you really do it because you want to be No. 1. That is something everybody understands. I was winning everything on clay in 1973, but I also knew that alone wouldn't automatically make me No. 1. I had to win on hard, grass or indoor courts as well to reach that level. It was good motivation."

By finishing 1973 as the No. 1 ranked player in the world, Nastase assured himself a place in the history books. He also entered a club even more exclusive than the fraternity of Grand Slam tournament winners.

Reflecting on that, he says: "When you're playing in a tournament you don't think about No. 1. I didn't realise what that might mean at the time because I was too busy just trying to survive day-to-day, week-to-week. I didn't really have much time to enjoy my top ranking when I had it, because everybody wanted to take it away from me. But it's something I can finally enjoy. I can just relax, look back, and think '**I did this, I was No. 1, and whatever happens after that doesn't matter or change the fact.**'"

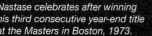

Nastase celebrates after winning his third consecutive year-end title at the Masters in Boston, 1973.

"That's the great thing about being No. 1 – everybody's after you"

By Peter Bodo

Jimmy Connors
1974 · 1975 · 1976 · 1977 · 1978

A native of the American heartland (Jimmy Connors was born in Illinois, just across the Mississippi River from St. Louis), he blew into professional tennis with the force of a Great Plains tornado – a whirling, swirling, hyper-aggressive baseliner with lethal, flat ground-strokes anchored by a two-handed backhand into which he flung his entire body with abandon. Connors earned worldwide recognition and respect for his competitive zeal, but what might have been even more remarkable was his ability to sustain that *joie de combat*; in a historic moment, he reached the semi-finals of the US Open in 1991, at age 39.

No player in ATP history can speak with more authority on the struggle to remain at the very top of the game. Connors was forced to surrender his top ranking nine times after he first hit No.1 - a battle that raged on for nearly a decade against men who were titans in the game: Bjorn Borg, John McEnroe, Ivan Lendl. Connors finished as the year-end No.1 for five consecutive years starting in 1974, and continued to challenge for that honour until deep into 1983. And he remained a force long after that, amassing a record 109 career singles titles – 15 more than his nearest rival, Ivan Lendl (94).

Given his reputation as the ultimate tennis warrior, the consummate irony is that he was, in what has become a famous phrase, '**Taught by women, to beat men**'. Those women were Connors' mother Gloria and his maternal grandmother, who shaped a game distinguished by a compact take-back and no-frills, nearly level swing – with two hands on the backhand to add oomph that the slender, almost scrawny young man lacked. Even as a fully developed adult, Connors stood just 5-foot-10 and weighed in at just 150 pounds – in boxing terms, he was a welterweight.

Gloria Connors recognised her son's quickness, and taught him to take the ball on the rise – the trademark of an opportunistic player who likes to force the action. Just as important, she drilled into her beloved '**Jimbo**' that the moment he stepped onto the court he needed to be merciless and unrelenting. He formed no friendships or close relationships with his peers. "We were just acquaintances," he says. "There was real meat in our rivalry, right to the core. It was serious stuff. I can't imagine McEnroe putting his arm around my shoulder to console me the way you sometimes see them do now."

When Connors was 16, Gloria reckoned she was finished shaping his unique game and shipped him off to Southern California, to the equivalent of finishing school under the tutelage of former pro player Pancho Segura. Yet throughout his career, Connors has said, whenever he felt something awry in his game, a 10-minute telephone call with Gloria was all the fix he needed.

Connors was just 18 when he recorded his first eye-opening triumph – a win over redoubtable Roy Emerson in 1970 at the Pacific Southwest Championships. The following year he attended UCLA and won the NCAA singles championship. He turned pro soon thereafter, but shocked the highly esteemed pioneers of pro tennis (men like Rod Laver, Arthur Ashe, and John Newcombe) by refusing to join the ATP and warring in general with the establishment. Connors blazed his own trail, egged on by his iconoclastic, lone-wolf manager, the late Bill Riordan. A gifted promoter, Riordan fueled Connors' already healthy '**us vs. them**' mentality.

Connors burst out in full stardom after cutting his teeth on a minor, breakaway tour partly organised by Riordan. He won his first Grand Slam title in 1974, and by the end of the year he'd become the first man to win three majors in the same year since Rod Laver. He also paid a stiff penalty for asserting his independence when he was locked out of the French Open - and denied the chance at a historic, calendar year Grand Slam.

Over the ensuing years, Connors won eight Grand Slam singles titles in 15 finals – despite playing the Australian Open just twice. He also became the first male to hold the No. 1 ranking

for 200 weeks (he finished with 268 weeks, fourth behind Roger Federer's record 302).

Curiously, Connors finished with a significant head-to-head disadvantage over his three storied rivals, Borg, McEnroe and Lendl. Connors was 35-57 against that group, but their relative youth (Borg was four years younger, Lendl nearly eight) as well as Connors longevity account for some of that disparity.

One thing, though, that's unaffected by those numbers, or any other ones, is Connors' legacy as a star in whom the competitor and showman reached full, equal expression. Connors consistently – and controversially - banged the drum for '**taking the game to the next level**' by rejecting all that was staid and gentlemanly about the game in favour of a more gladiatorial approach. He became famous for his outlandish comments, among them:

- "I'll chase… Borg to the ends of the earth. I'll be waiting for him. I'll dog him everywhere. Every time he looks around he'll see my shadow." (Uttered after Connors was beaten by Borg at Wimbledon, and then asked if he would travel to Australia at the end of the year [the tournament was played in December then]

if it meant preventing a Borg Grand Slam.)

- "If the sun rose and set on Wimbledon, a lot of guys wouldn't have a suntan." (Said after a loss at Wimbledon, where Connors was a two-time champion in six finals).

- "New Yorkers love it when you spill your guts out there. Spill your guts at Wimbledon and they make you stop and clean it up."

- "This is what they came for, this is what they want." (Connors shouted those words into a courtside camera, his face right up against the lens, in the midst of his astonishing comeback against Aaron Krickstein in that magical 1991 US Open).

Large numbers of fans also were appalled by Connors' vulgarity and his crude and rude gestures and comments, but the one thing the majority of them had in common with his ardent supporters was a respect for Connors the competitor. As he says, "The one thing I was prepared. I gave it everything I had, every time I walked out on the court. I was never unprepared, or willing to just let it go. I gave the fans their money's worth."

Bjorn Borg
1979 · 1980

By Peter Bodo

As impressive as his numerous accomplishments and records are, Bjorn Borg will also be remembered as a seminal figure in the cultural history of the Open Era and the ATP. His career prefigured the age of the cradle-to-grave tennis pro, and he ushered in the era of the European superstar.

Borg was also the first tennis player to shine as brightly as a rock star in pop cultural galaxy.

Born and raised in the small Swedish town of Södertälje, Borg would become the greatest of all clay-court players – by far – until the emergence of Rafael Nadal. But Borg's proficiency on grass, his relatively compact strokes, and the dominant role of quickness in his game point to a counter-intuitive aspect of his development. "You know, growing up in Sweden meant we had a lot of rain," he says. "We were taught on clay courts but because of the weather (and seasonal obstacles), we had to go indoors (on faster surfaces) - a lot."

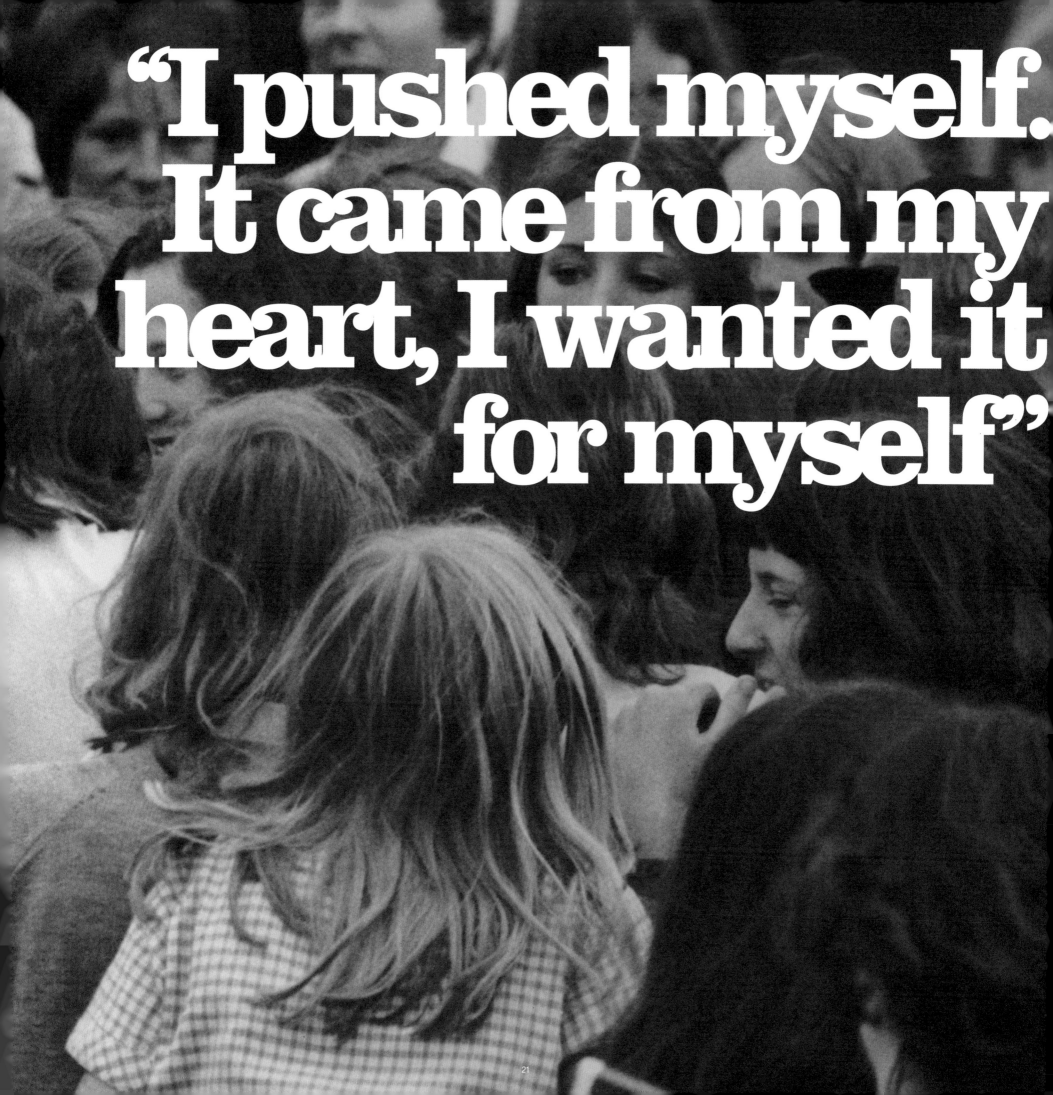

"I pushed myself. It came from my heart, I wanted it for myself"

"We're playing tennis, but Bjorn - he's playing something else"

Ilie Nastase

"Those who have been No. 1, they are the ones who, when it comes to five-all in the fifth set, are winning those important points. A lot of people can get to five-all in the fifth, but it is what you do then. That is the difference between top 100, 50, 10... and then the very top. It is hard to explain why some can't and others can. You have to be so strong mentally."

Borg and an eight-year-old future No. 1 Andre Agassi.

Young Bjorn's precocity was such that his extreme topspin strokes, hit with a wrenching wrist action reminiscent of table tennis, were natural and tamper-proof by the time he was 13. Borg's radical style, combined with his athleticism, led Nastase to say, "We're playing tennis, but Bjorn – he's playing something else."

Borg was beating the best under-18 players in Sweden before he turned 14, and was so clearly destined for global stardom that he was taken under the wing of the man who would remain his career-long coach, former Swedish Davis Cup captain Lennart Bergelin.

By the time Borg turned 14 he was travelling the international circuit with Bergelin, a full-fledged tennis pro. And he was doing it because he – not a pushy parent or overly ambitious coach – wanted to do it. "I had good people around me - good parents - coaches, but there was no one pushing me," he says. "I pushed myself. It came from my heart, I wanted it for myself."

Many youngsters 'want it', but Borg's ability

to get it, and almost immediately, remains unparalleled. He won his first Davis Cup match at 15, and his first Grand Slam title (at Roland Garros, 1974) when he was barely 18. He developed rapidly into a magnificent physical specimen; fleet as an antelope, he was lean but muscular, with shoulders so wide they made his chest look almost concave. Borg had a resting heart rate of about 50 beats-per-minute (compared to the human average of 60-100), but his greatest assets probably were his mental and emotional focus and self-control – qualities that enabled him to play his best and most lethal tennis when it most mattered.

"You are born with certain things," he says, pondering his astonishing early success, "But the mentality - tennis is such a mental sport - it is very difficult and that is a learning process when you are young. Some players never reach the top because of the mental thing."

Borg would repeat as the French Open champion in 1975, then the following year he also solved the Wimbledon challenge. Between

1978 and 1981, he was in every final at Roland Garros and Wimbledon. Adriano Panatta, who defeated Borg in the fourth round in 1973 and again in the quarter-finals in '76, would remain the only player ever to beat Borg at Roland Garros. Borg won a grand total of six French Open titles and five consecutive Wimbledon finals starting in 1976. Nobody has come close to equalling his record of back-to-back victories at the French Open and Wimbledon three years running (1978-80).

The record Borg left behind is unique in a number of ways, and begs to be quantified. Borg won 39.3 percent of all the Grand Slam tournaments he entered, and his winning percentage across all tour events and surfaces was 82.7 percent. Yet he had a puzzling aversion to the US Open (he lost in four finals) and only played once at the Australian Open.

Borg's remarkable exploits exacted a price. Borg quit the game in 1981 not long after he turned 25 (a brief comeback attempt in 1992 ended badly - if quickly – after one

tournament), by which time he'd been playing on the pro tour for a little over nine years – and fighting a running skirmish for the No. 1 ranking with rivals Jimmy Connors and John McEnroe for four years. Borg was the year-end No. 1 for two years, 1979 and 1980. "When you are a kid you have dreams, like winning Wimbledon, but to be No. 1, that's something different. I remember when I was there it was a great feeling. It is a terrific achievement; it is just so difficult to do. It was tough – very tough."

Borg's life was complicated by the fact that he triggered something very much like the sporting culture's equivalent to Beatlemania. With his flowing blond locks and almost androgynous appeal, Borg was described often as a 'teen angel', and he was often called a 'rock star' of tennis. He needed a police escort as he made his way around the grounds at Wimbledon. At the French Open, he was photographed jumping out of a locker room window to escape the hordes of young girls hoping to ambush him at the players' exit.

"He was bigger than the game. He was like Elvis or Liz Taylor or somebody"

Arthur Ashe

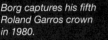

Borg captures his fifth Roland Garros crown in 1980.

"I wanted to win, even in practice"

Bjorn Borg

It's hard to describe the conflicts and stress this must have created in a healthy young man who also embraced a Spartan regimen of training and practice in near isolation with his ever present mentor, coach and confidant, Bergelin. Whatever urge Borg had to rebel, to enjoy the fruits and advantages afforded by his success, were effectively suppressed for long years, and that grated on Borg – and it certainly contributed to his decision to escape the sport that had become his gilded cage.

"It's tough when you're No.1. You don't have any private life, you can't even walk anywhere," he says. "I think that was one reason why I lost my motivation to play tennis."

The motivation vanished, and more comprehensively and irrevocably than anyone imagined when Borg simply dropped his racquets and walked away after the US Open of 1981 – mere weeks after he had turned over his No.1 ranking to McEnroe. But the Borg legacy will endure, as will his role in the evolution of the game.

"You don't get tired of being No. 1"

John McEnroe

1981 · 1982 · 1983 · 1984

By Peter Bodo

When John Patrick McEnroe was in second grade at St. Anastasia's Catholic elementary school in New York City, a teacher told his parents John and Kay that their son was gifted, and suggested that they should consider making whatever sacrifice was necessary to get young John into a good private school.

The teacher was right, only she couldn't know at the time that John's greatest gifts lay outside the schoolhouse door – in that marvellously attuned nervous system, in that acutely sensitive left hand, and – most difficult to anticipate – in that fierce urge for perfection.

McEnroe would develop those gifts swiftly and parlay them into one of the most remarkable of tennis careers, even by the dizzying standard of the ATP's elite. Only three other year-end No. 1s in ATP history finished in the top position for four consecutive years: Jimmy Connors, Pete Sampras and Roger Federer. And not a single one of them can match McEnroe's versatility and success in enterprises other than tournament singles.

McEnroe with doubles partner Peter Fleming. McEnroe would finish as the year-end No.1 doubles player for five consecutive years from 1979 - 1983.

McEnroe captures his first Wimbledon crown in 1981 with victory over Borg.

McEnroe helped the United States win five Davis Cups – he's the greatest player ever to represent the most successful nation in that competition. He also found the time and energy to win nine Grand Slam doubles titles - seven with his regular partner Peter Fleming, who famously said, when asked to name the greatest doubles team of all time: "John McEnroe and anybody."

McEnroe finished as the No.1 doubles player for five years, three of them concurrent with his top singles ranking. "People never seem to mention that," McEnroe says. Breaking out that famous, crooked grin, he adds: "Hey, add the singles and doubles together and tally up the weeks and I'd even blow past Roger (Federer)!"

McEnroe's humour, wry and self-deprecating, is just one of the many things that tennis types couldn't really appreciate until after he stowed his racquets and became a widely popular television commentator and tennis ambassador-at-large. "I'm happy I've had a pretty successful second career," he says. "Every top player has to be a certain unique way to succeed, and when I was in the thick of it people would just see this anger, this effort and intensity. That was my way. People didn't see that maybe I didn't take myself quite as seriously as it appeared."

McEnroe's raging perfectionism was at least partly responsible for some of the most famous temperamental outbursts and meltdowns in tennis history – thanks to McEnroe, '**pits of the world**' and '**You cannot be serious!**' are staples of the tennis lexicon. But for many, even his inexcusable excesses seemed at least understandable - in context. For McEnroe's early biography might have been titled, '**Portrait of the Artist as a Young Tennis Player**'.

That left-handed game of McEnroe's was radically original, from the back-to-the-net, corkscrewing service action to that oddly restrained forehand drive, to the volley so deft that if you threw an egg over the net at him, he likely could have returned it without breaking the shell.

At the time McEnroe burst onto the scene in 1977, qualifying for Wimbledon and reaching the semi-finals in just his second major tournament, the game was ruled by Sweden's Bjorn Borg and McEnroe's countryman, Jimmy Connors. Within months, McEnroe emerged as their challenger and the game - already simmering in the public imagination - boiled over. "I take unbelievable satisfaction in being part of something important to tennis history," he says. "That time, the late 1970s and early 1980s was, and still is, magical to me."

McEnroe hit No.1 in just his fourth year on the circuit, soon after he turned 21, and lasted there just three weeks. Although he'd earned the ranking and had his first Grand Slam title by then, Borg stood in his way. In 1981, Borg won the French Open, but McEnroe then avenged his 1980 loss to Borg in the Wimbledon final. Thus, the 1981 US Open final between the two boiled down to a battle for the year-end No.1 ranking – and McEnroe took it.

"That's when it dawned on me that it was a passing of the guard," McEnroe recalls. "There was suddenly more pressure, everywhere. The difference between being ranked No.2 and No.1 is enormous in the way you're covered and watched, the recognition factor, all the things you have to deal with.

McEnroe defeats Borg in 1981 US Open final. It was to be the Swede's last Grand Slam match.

"I take unbelievable satisfaction in being part of something important to tennis history."

"Arguably, the most fun years of my career were when I was moving up. I've heard lots of guys say that all they cared about was winning Grand Slams. My position always was different. I put a lot more emphasis on finishing the year as high as possible. I was more into the idea that tennis wasn't about two or three tournaments, it was about a full season. It was about consistency. And in those years, tennis was virtually a year-round season."

That attitude helps explain why McEnroe worked so hard to hang onto that year-end No.1 ranking, and how, in a concentrated six-year period, he managed to win seven Grand Slam singles titles - all at Wimbledon and the US Open. McEnroe's one failure haunts him to this day: he never did win the French Open, and missed his best chance when he let a two-sets-to-love lead over his rival Ivan

Lendl slip away in the 1984 final. It added a lasting, bittersweet element to a historic year in which McEnroe recorded the best single-year winning percentage in singles in ATP history (he was 82-3, for a 96.47 winning percentage).

Although he failed to win another major in singles in the eight years following that spectacular 1984, he continued to flesh out other portions of his résumé to emerge as the most versatile player in ATP history. He was truly a player's player, and a competitor's competitor.

That second grade teacher turned out to be right, although she probably could not have guessed in just what way it would be.

1973 - 1984
In Focus

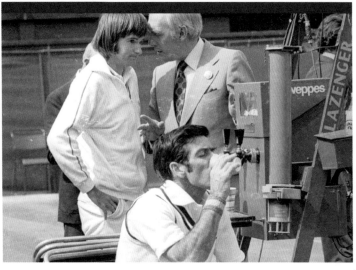

Left: Romanian Ilie Nastase - noted for his 'sorcery' with the racquet.

Above: Ken Rosewall, at 39, gets ready to take on 21-year-old American Jimmy Connors in the 1974 Wimbledon final.

Above Right: Arthur Ashe - one of the founders of the ATP - became President of the organisation in 1974.

Top Right: Guillermo Vilas puts together a record 46-match winning streak in 1977.

Bottom Right: Bjorn Borg enjoys success over Victor Pecci in the Roland Garros final, June 1979.

1973

The ATP establishes the computer ranking system, providing a fair analysis of a player's performance and creating an objective way to determine entries into tournaments.

August 23: Ilie Nastase becomes the first No. 1 player. Nastase captures a remarkable 14 titles throughout the season. He finishes the season by capturing his third straight Masters title with a four-set win over Dutchman Tom Okker in Boston.

1974 - '75

The Men's International Professional Tennis Council (MIPTC), made up of ATP, ILTF and tournament directors, is formed to govern the sport as an independent, democratic, international body for the administration of professional tennis.

June 3: John Newcombe becomes No. 1 at 30 years, 12 days (the oldest first-time No. 1 player to this day).

July 29: 21-year-old Jimmy Connors becomes the first American to rank No. 1. In his first tournament in top spot at the US Clay Court Championships in Indianapolis, Connors beats 18-year-old Bjorn Borg for the first time and finishes the season at No. 1, winning four of his last five events.

Connors captures three Grand Slams that year, including his first triumph at Wimbledon in which he defeats Australian Ken Rosewall in the final. It was to be Rosewall's fourth and final runner-up finish at Wimbledon, the first coming an incredible 20 years prior, in 1954.

Arthur Ashe is elected as the ATP's second president in 1974 (serving until mid-1979).

1976 - '78

The ATP Doubles computer rankings begin on March 1, 1976.

Connors holds the singles No. 1 ranking for 160 consecutive weeks but on August 23, 1977, Borg takes over No. 1 for the first time, for one week only. Connors, Borg and Argentine Guillermo Vilas, a winner at Roland Garros and the US Open in 1977, captivate fans worldwide with a three-way rivalry at the top of the game that year. Despite a record 46-match winning streak from Vilas in '77, Connors holds the No. 1 ranking for 84 consecutive weeks and finishes as the year-end No. 1 five years in a row from 1974-78.

Borg, a winner at Roland Garros and Wimbledon in 1978, had established himself as the biggest threat to Connors' reign.

1979 - 80

In a ground-breaking move, four young Chinese players compete in US tournaments for the first time in over 21 years after being sponsored by the ATP.

April 9, 1979: Borg takes over No. 1. And having completed the Roland Garros – Wimbledon 'double' for a second consecutive year, Borg finishes as year-end No. 1 for the first time in '79.

Borg relinquishes the top spot to John McEnroe, who, just a couple of weeks after his 21st birthday, takes over No. 1 on March 3, 1980. The left-handed New Yorker beats rival Jimmy Connors in the Memphis final in two tie-break sets to seal his rise to No. 1.

March 24, 1980: Borg regains No. 1. A burgeoning rivalry between Borg and McEnroe reaches a climax when the two engage in a 1980 Wimbledon final that would transcend the sport. Borg triumphs in five sets to capture a fifth consecutive Wimbledon title.

The Swede finishes as year-end No. 1 for the second season in a row.

1981

July 6: One day after winning his first Wimbledon crown over rival Borg, McEnroe returns to No. 1.

Later that summer, the American takes a solid hold of No. 1 and wins the ATP Championship in Cincinnati leading into the US Open where he wins for a third straight year, defeating Borg in the final. It would be the final meeting between McEnroe and Borg, who had played his last Grand Slam match.

McEnroe finishes as year-end No. 1 for the first time in his career.

1982

September 13: Connors, at age 30, regains No. 1 after capturing his fourth US Open title. Connors holds the top spot for seven weeks before McEnroe closes the season with four consecutive indoor titles (San Francisco, Sydney, Tokyo, Wembley).

McEnroe takes over the top spot on November 15 and closes with his second year-end No. 1 finish.

1983

More changes at No. 1 occur during the 1983 season than in any other season in the history of the Emirates ATP Rankings. There are a total of 10 changes at No. 1, with three players battling it out (Connors, Lendl and McEnroe) during the season.

February 28: 22-year-old Lendl becomes the sixth No. 1 and the only player from the Czech Republic to hold the world's top ranking.

July 4: On American Independence Day, McEnroe takes a firm grip on No. 1 after winning his second Wimbledon title. He would hold the top position for 17 weeks, the most all season.

October 31: After winning the Tokyo-indoor title, Lendl makes a late season charge to become No. 1 for six weeks before McEnroe takes it back on December 12, the latest date of a No. 1 change in the history of the Emirates ATP Rankings.

1984

The No. 1 ranking would alternate between Lendl and McEnroe seven times during the year as both players dominated the Tour.

Lendl briefly returns to the top position for one week (on June 11) following his breakthrough win at Roland Garros, a triumph that would end McEnroe's 42-match winning streak.

Yet McEnroe would not be denied the year-end No. 1 ranking that year. The American compiles an incredible 82-3 campaign throughout the season, counting wins at Wimbledon, the US Open as well as the Masters in his hometown of New York City over his rival Lendl.

McEnroe finishes as No. 1 for a fourth consecutive year.

"I was between 2 and 3 in the world for two, three years. That's not exactly where I wanted to be"

Ivan Lendl
1985 · 1986 · 1987 · 1989

By Neil Harman

The news reached Ivan Lendl while he was on a Davis Cup errand for Czechoslovakia in Paraguay in the first week of March, 1983. He recalls a short and abrupt sensation. He thought it was a fluke. The No.1 ranking was dashed from him within a week and he got back down to work as if nothing had happened. And that was what made Lendl appreciably different.

As time went on, Lendl's junior potential transferred fully to achievement at tour level. And then, thanks to a splash of Grand Slam titles that began in the unpromising circumstance of trailing John McEnroe by two sets-to-love in the final of Roland Garros in 1984, Lendl would reach the summit once more. This time, he was willing to accept that he merited the accolade.

ProTennis

The official newspaper of World Championship Tennis

Volume 3, Number 3   *ProTennis, January 21, 1982*

A giant step for Steve Denton

Dieting Texan improves ranking by 416 places

By JOHN PARSONS
Special Correspondent

BIRMINGHAM, Eng. — One miserably damp morning in Chichester, an English town on the South coast, better known for its theatre than its tennis, an unmistakably overweight young American was to be seen at just about noon pulling and panting around the local soccer ground.

Doubles warmed up the

Lendl defeats McEnroe in the 1985 Roland Garros final to capture his first Grand Slam title.

Lendl holds the Masters trophy aloft at Madison Square Garden. He was to capture the year-end title five times whilst it was held in New York.

Lendl celebrates after beating John McEnroe in the 1985 US Open final.

In one sense, there was hardly a tennis player who more deserved the plaudits that came with being the best at what he did, and yet none for whom the accordant fame sat less easily. Lendl did what he did because it was there to be done. He strove harder than anyone else [at that time], which made his opponents uneasy and left the public largely bathed in apathy. Fixated with being the best that he could be, the No.1 ranking would come if he did all that needed to be done. The rest was frippery.

The manner of rising to the top of the rankings was simple, in Lendl's mind. Win the major trophies and the rest of the pieces would fall into place. It was, therefore, when he won the 1985 US Open, his second major triumph, defeating McEnroe once more in the final and was cemented into the position of the best at what he did, that Lendl was ready to concede that he deserved it.

That final was recalled in Sports Illustrated by the brilliant Frank Deford: "Apart from a walking start, his defeat of McEnroe was awesome. Lendl, who has been studying under Tony Roche, the past master of the volley, won from the net as well as from the baseline. Curiously, McEnroe won his first 16 points on service, broke Lendl the first time he served, had a set point at 5-2 and served for the set at 5-3. But, suddenly, the match turned, and Lendl started thinking, 'There's no ball I can't get to, and no shot I can't hit.'"

It was to stay like that in Lendl's career – aside of his vain attempts to win Wimbledon – until his back gave in and he could not play anymore. He would be the best player in the world for 270 weeks [over five years] which most people thought would stand for all time, until Pete Sampras and Roger Federer broke it.

"Did I strive to be No.1? I never did," he said. "I always thought that being No.1 should be a by-product of winning majors. If you go after No.1 and you don't win a major, a) it doesn't mean that much and b) you're going to be the subject of the matters that have affected those players who reach that status without a major, which involves having to deal with all sorts of difficult questions from you guys [the press].

"Don't get me wrong, it is a great achievement. I'm saying if you do well in the majors you're going to take care of it and winning the majors was always more important.

"If you want to win as many majors as possible, there's always the next one in a few months. If you reach No.1 and are satisfied, you are in danger of slumping down. From what I've read or heard, it could be [that way] for certain players.

"Some of the nicest memories I have from the tour was beating Bjorn [Borg] and then Jose-Luis Clerc to win the Swiss Open in Basel, which is a small tournament compared to the majors but those were two good matches and I have a tremendous feeling of satisfaction from them - and beating Borg any time anywhere was always good."

There were a total of 94 '**satisfactions**' in Lendl's storied career, eight of which came in those championships that accorded him the greatest of all sensations, though one would elude him. "In 1990, I played Key Biscayne and nothing else until Queen's [skipping the entire clay court season including the French Open] because I wanted to win Wimbledon so much. I knew I would have kept the No.1 ranking longer had I played all that time and, perhaps, that record would have stayed for longer. It was a price I was happy to pay."

"I became No. 1 and I was more than a tennis player"

Mats Wilander
1988

By Neil Harman

Mats Wilander was not chasing the dream - he was pursuing the man. The man was Ivan Lendl. To get to be the best, he had to copy the best and in 1988, a lot earlier than he thought was possible, Wilander snagged his prey in the final of the US Open. For a short while, he became the finest there was. Looking back now, he still cannot believe it turned out the way it did.

The Swede had won his first Grand Slam at the age of 17 in Paris, though he did not possess the magnetism of Bjorn Borg, nor the silky talent of Stefan Edberg and was therefore difficult to pigeon-hole. He was the progressive thinker, the political rebel. He was a deft and calculated player who methodically spun his web. He was not a headline-grabber.

Wilander defeats Lendl
64 46 63 57 64 in the 1988
US Open final and secures
the No. 1 ranking.

"The goal was to beat
Lendl, to become so strong
that you feel invincible,
he was the target and he
happened to be No. 1 at the
time and hard courts were
the one place I couldn't
beat him. The day after, it
was over. I knew I was the
best player in the world.
But I wasn't the best
player in the world after
winning that match, I was
the best before that match,
but we just hadn't played
each other."

Wilander remembers being told by his physical trainer, Matt Doyle, that playing a lot of tennis and running in the woods was not going to make him any stronger or quicker. And that, if he was going to catch Lendl, he had to have a much better, more coordinated plan.

"Matt told me I could run forever but I needed a percentage here and there and I lost to Lendl three times in 1987, in the final of the French, of the US and the Masters and it was going in the wrong direction. He was kicking my ass. In '88, it all changed, Lendl lost to [Pat] Cash in the semi-finals of the Australian and I got lucky to beat [Stefan] Edberg in five and Cash in five and I was starting to feel 'wow this is happening'. And then Lendl and I somehow avoided one another for almost the whole of '88. I couldn't really focus on the smaller events because I was working too hard physically and in the middle of the Open, I suddenly realised if we both get to the final, we are playing for the No.1 ranking.

"I won Cincinnati and it was perfect. This is what I've been working for. The hard thing was to focus on getting to the final, I just wanted these people out of my way. I just wanted Lendl. He was the No.1 and he had been for a while and this was his seventh final in a row. It wasn't a big deal for him, I knew that. But I didn't know if he was playing well or bad, I hadn't played him for a while and it was a huge deal for me. It was the US Open, no Swede had ever won it. I was living in Greenwich, Connecticut, where he lived. I practised at his home because he had a court just like the one at Flushing Meadows and I had a court built at my home as well. On the days off, like him, I'd not go into New York, but practise at home. I took the whole thing from him."

The final would turn out to be the longest on record, an attritional battle, four hours and 54 minutes, and when Wilander won it, he had become the top man in tennis. He stayed up all night, visited his favourite bar, Bill's on 54th Street, went on the David Letterman show, and briefly, felt so strong that nothing could touch him. And then, as he said, the balloon just popped.

"I was going to play the Olympics in Seoul and decided not to. In 1987, 1988, I was politically involved in tennis. I had moved to Monaco, met my wife in New York City. I was a little kid from Sweden and I suddenly became a New York City guy, where fashion, rock 'n roll and tennis went together, but with that came a rebellious mind-set. I became No.1 and I was more than a tennis player in my mind and I lost track of what my goals really were because it happened so quickly. I was aiming at 1990, '91 [to be No.1] not '88.

Winning three majors in '88 was never a goal. After the Open, I went to Palermo, there were a lot of bodyguards because I was No.1, 'oh cool bodyguards'. I beat Kent Carlsson in the final on clay and I did that because I was No.1. That was the only tournament I played feeling like I was No.1. I played the way I did at the US Open, I served and volleyed, sliced, played drop shots with a cocky attitude and it worked.

"From there, though I worked real hard in 1989 and '90 - harder than before - as soon as I played matches, I didn't know what I was doing. The picture wasn't clear. I wasn't good enough to go in there and bully an opponent which is what these other guys could do. My brain was my weapon, but that was tired so I lost matches. It was over and I never felt that again."

Wilander celebrates his seventh and final Grand Slam victory, at the 1988 US Open.

"The best thing about it is telling your kids you were No. 1"

Stefan Edberg
1990 · 1991

By Peter Bodo

For an extended period early in his career, sceptics suggested that while Stefan Edberg had a glorious serve-and-volley game ideally suited to the quick grass courts at Wimbledon, the phlegmatic Swede didn't have the kind of '**fire in the belly**' (the phrase used by his long-term coach Tony Pickard) that would drive him to achieve the ultimate honour - reaching the No. 1 ranking and holding it through the end of a calendar year.

It turned out that the diffident Edberg – a latter-day incarnation of the '**sporting gentleman**' of yore – had more than enough competitive fire smouldering in his nether regions, and he didn't need a Lucifer from the enormous stick-match factory in his home town of Västervik to light it. And it certainly didn't hurt Edberg's cause that he also had a cool, analytical mind that helped him survive the constant pressure with which the risk-taking serve-and-volleyer must live.

Edberg and Becker prepare to face off in the first of three consecutive Wimbledon finals, in 1988.

Born in the quiet town of Västervik, Sweden, Edberg first captured the imagination of the tennis establishment in 1983, when he completed a '**junior Grand Slam**' by winning all four major titles in the under-18 age division. He was just 17 at the time, and before he turned 19 he had won his first ATP tournament as well as a gold medal when tennis was re-introduced to the Olympic Games - as a demonstration sport in Los Angeles.

By then, Edberg had developed the tools that would vault him to the top of the game, starting with his signature stroke: that explosive kick serve that he relied on almost exclusively to set up those deft, razor-sharp volleys with which he cut opponents to ribbons.

Edberg also had an elegant, highly reliable one-handed backhand that he employed offensively or defensively, with either slice or topspin, and a somewhat odd-looking forehand that put a final touch on one of the truly unique – and lethal – games of the Open Era.

Edberg won his first Grand Slam singles title at the Australian Open in 1985 (at the time, the tournament was held in late December). He defended that title successfully, and would go on to win five more major singles titles (and two in doubles) as well as the season-ending Masters (1989). All told, he won 42 singles titles and played on three teams that won the Davis Cup.

At the peak of his career Edberg also engaged Boris Becker in one of the great Wimbledon rivalries of all time; he faced the German idol in three successive finals (1988-90), winning two of them. The rubber match, destined to live on in Wimbledon lore and legend, was the last of those clashes. Edberg was down a break in the fifth set in that one but he managed to pull out the win.

Never entirely comfortable in the limelight, Edberg was no nakedly ambitious player bent on becoming No.1. "That wasn't so much of an ambition, it wasn't something I fantasised about when I was young," he says now. "I just wanted to be the best in my age group. But by the age of 16, I began to aim a little higher, mainly because Mats Wilander (a contemporary and rival who was a year-and-a-half older) won the French Open before he turned 18. So I started dreaming about the French Open."

Ironically, the French Open was the one Grand Slam that would elude Edberg.

Pundits often found the young Edberg enigmatic, and suspected his dispassionate manner. This was a quiet kid whose response to losing before the championship match at Wimbledon one year was a shrug and the dry comment, "Well, I'm still in the doubles." He seemed to have a moth-and-flame relationship with success.

"I don't think I really thought about the year-end No.1 ranking much," he recalls. "For two or three years I was a Grand Slam champion but not the No.1. I didn't realise the importance of it until late in my career."

Inevitably, though, Edberg closed on the No.1 ranking during the sweltering heat and humidity in the American heartland city of Cincinnati in August 1990. At the Masters 1000 tournament there, he needed a quarter-final win over gritty, defensive baseline specialist Michael Chang to clinch the top ranking. Edberg survived a grueling duel, 6-4 in the third – whereupon he celebrated in typical Edbergian fashion: "We (Pickard and Edberg) had a little champagne that night. It was unusual. We just had a little."

That historic win was part of a remarkable 21-match winning streak that came to a grinding halt at the US Open a few weeks later, when the newly crowned No.1 became the first top seed in tournament history to lose in the first round. Critics pounced on him, suggesting that he lacked fire to win in tough, gritty New York, and couldn't handle

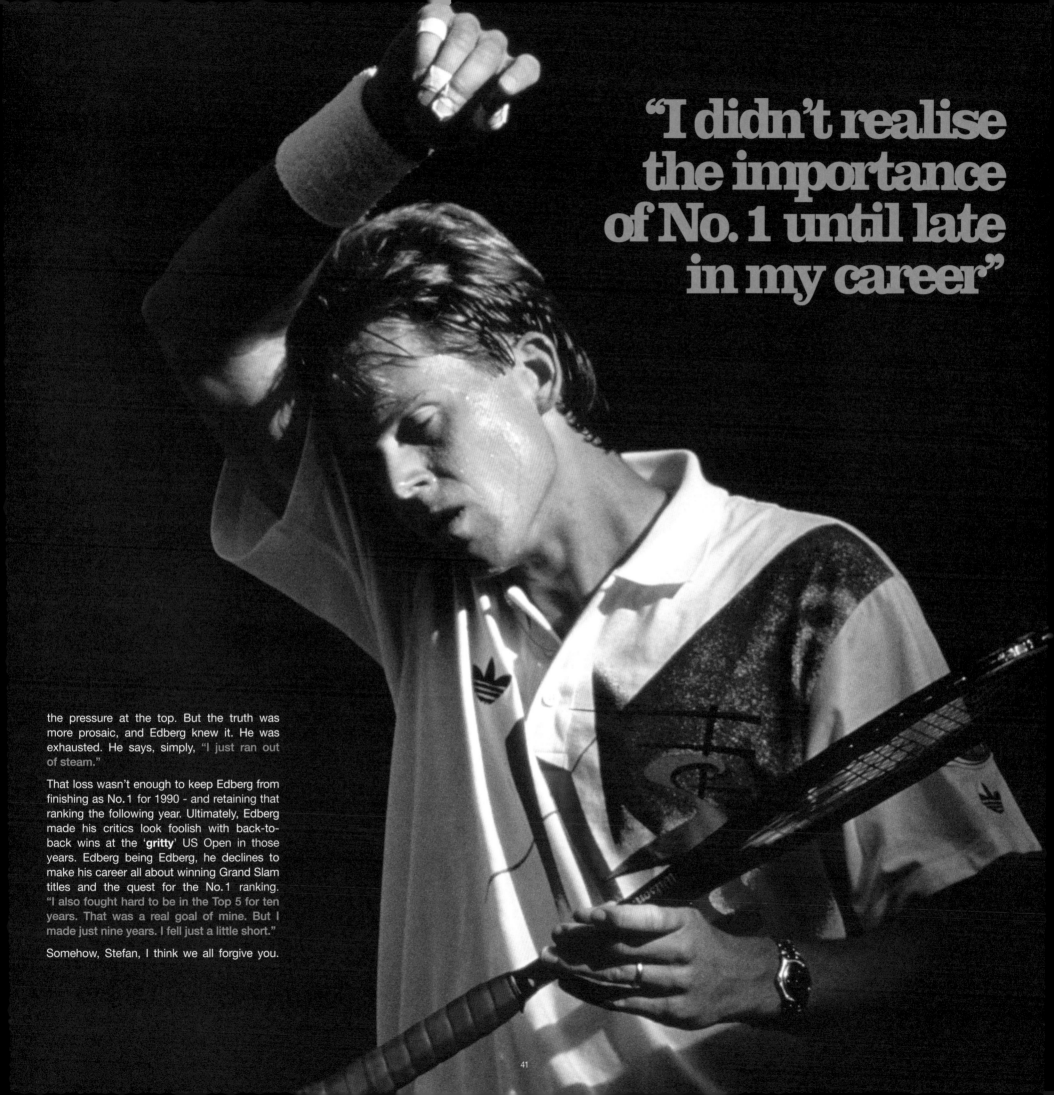

"I didn't realise the importance of No. 1 until late in my career"

the pressure at the top. But the truth was more prosaic, and Edberg knew it. He was exhausted. He says, simply, "I just ran out of steam."

That loss wasn't enough to keep Edberg from finishing as No.1 for 1990 - and retaining that ranking the following year. Ultimately, Edberg made his critics look foolish with back-to-back wins at the 'gritty' US Open in those years. Edberg being Edberg, he declines to make his career all about winning Grand Slam titles and the quest for the No.1 ranking. "I also fought hard to be in the Top 5 for ten years. That was a real goal of mine. But I made just nine years. I fell just a little short."

Somehow, Stefan, I think we all forgive you.

"There are very few things in life that get to follow you and this is one of them"

Jim Courier

1992

By Neil Harman

For Jim Courier, it was not the increasing global range of men's tennis that made reaching No. 1 in the world so strenuous, there were three players from his own nation forever ahead of him and who, he felt, possessed superior claims. "Pete Sampras, Andre Agassi and Michael Chang were always being touted and deservedly so," Courier said. "To outside observers and from my own lens my game was not appealing the way theirs was. I wasn't offended by it. In fact, I was fuelled by it in some respects. It didn't bother me that being No. 1 wasn't the foregone conclusion in the way it was for other players."

And so Courier did what he always did, he buckled down, he worked himself to the bone, he developed an extra layer of hardness [if that was possible] and made certain that he would try to rein them in, one by one, until he could not be denied.

"The shot that got me to No. 1? I think I hit a volley. I've never watched the tape. I think my grandmother gave it to me, and it's laying in a closet somewhere. Fewer people get to No. 1 and the emotion I felt was equal to winning a major if not greater."

Coach Jose Higueras helped Courier to four
Grand Slam titles and the No. 1 ranking.

Then, on a February night in San Francisco in 1992 – with the Australian Open just pocketed and the French Open already on his résumé – it all came together for the 21-year-old Floridian. He needed to make the final of the tournament run by the late Barry McKay, to overtake a non-American, Stefan Edberg, who was in pole position. Three of the four matches he played that week went to three sets - he came from a set down in two, including his semi-final victory over Derrick Rostagno that accorded Courier his seminal ranking moment.

"I was stressed out about it, an indoor tournament, not my best surface. And I was very aware of the situation and I was also aware I might not get there because Edberg was playing in Brussels the week after that, the points were very close and I just wanted to get there for one week, just to say I'd been to the top of the mountain," Courier said. "It's something I'd never remotely dreamed of. It's not as if I was one of these kids who was told from the beginning **'you're great, you're great, you're going to be a champion'**; there were always players around me who were better than me and I worked my way into it and got myself into a position, and hit a sweet spot and found myself there so it was an incredibly exciting and tense week."

"It wasn't a major or a Masters, I didn't have to beat the protagonists to get it, but Rostagno was wildly unpredictable and very dangerous particularly on a greasy indoor court. He was prone to anything including beating himself. We went three sets and I toughed it out and I remember going down to my knees, this is it, this is the moment, they can never take it away from me."

Courier, now regarded as one of the sport's leading commentators and interviewers, struggled to summon the words to quantify what reaching this particular peak meant to him – "you would have to use some kind of chemical to check my adrenalin levels before and after to realise what it meant. Such a relief and rush, I was completely flattened. Basically since I left Australia, I had thought about nothing except getting to the finals, and the air went out of the balloon in a massive way."

Courier recalls being **'smoked'** in the final the following day by Chang but that nothing could ever diminish his sense of achievement. Then he was scheduled to fly to Brussels to fulfil corporate obligations and to play in the tournament which in itself became a novel adventure. He had missed the overnight flight from San Francisco to London, instead took the red eye to New York and would then fly supersonic to Britain and connect on to Belgium. "We were on Concorde, heading to the runway but we backed up, the nose wheel wouldn't turn, the flight was cancelled so I spent my first full day as the No.1 player, ordering pizza, sitting in an airport lounge with strangers, with my agent and girlfriend."

Courier, who collected 23 titles and four Grand Slams along the way, was not a streaky player, he was not someone who rose and fell. Instead he was the epitome of consistency, who would offer steadfast endurance, a grinding efficiency and never take the comfortable route. Even his hold on the No.1 position was tenuous. He never felt entirely settled there. "Being No.1 is not something you wake up in the morning and look in the mirror and say **'Whoa, No.1 it's a great day.**' It is around and you are aware of it but you still have to go through all the same steps if you compete and try to retain it. It was all gravy for me, all upside, a dream come true. You hold on as long as you can, and if someone takes it, it's a bit like being President of the United States, it is the office, not the person who has the power."

Courier celebrates a five-set victory over fellow American Andre Agassi in the 1991 Roland Garros final.

1985 - 1992
In Focus

Left: Boris Becker serves at Wimbledon, 1985.

Above: *Ivan Lendl poses with the trophy at Roland Garros on June 8, 1986. Lendl defeated Mikael Pernfors in three sets.*

Right: *At the 1988 US Open, ATP CEO Hamilton Jordan (pictured), held the now-famous 'press conference in the parking lot'.*

1985

A worldwide star is born by the name of Germany's Boris Becker, who takes the tennis world by storm by capturing the Wimbledon title at the tender age of 17.

August 19: Lendl ends McEnroe's 53-week stretch at No.1. The American would regain the top spot going into the US Open. This would become the final two weeks at No.1 in his career. Lendl would capture his second career Grand Slam title at the US Open, finishing as year-end No.1 for the first time his career.

At the request of the ATP, MIPTC passes a Drug Testing Rule, making tennis the first professional sport to institute a workable and well-designed drug-testing programme.

1986 - 87

Lendl's run of 157 straight weeks at No.1 is the third-longest in the history of the Emirates ATP Rankings.

During his uninterrupted streak, Lendl puts almost identical back-to-back match records together of 74-6 (nine titles) in '86 and 74-7 (eight titles) in '87.

1988

The players, under ATP CEO Hamilton Jordan, hold a press conference in the US Open parking lot to announce that they will assume more control of the game. '**Tennis at the Crossroads**' outlines a plan for players to form a new Tour in which they would play a major role and bear greater responsibility for the future of the sport. The idea is quickly embraced by the membership. Eighty-five of the Top 100 ranked players sign a letter of support for a new Tour within weeks of the news conference. Tournament directors representing many of the world's leading events voice their support for the players and join them in what was to become a partnership unique in professional sports - players and tournaments each with an equal voice in how the circuit is run.

September 12: Mats Wilander becomes the second Swede (behind Borg) to hold the No.1 ranking, following a dramatic five-set win over Lendl in the US Open final. He finishes the season as No.1 with three Grand Slam crowns (Australian Open, Roland Garros, US Open).

Above Left: Ivan Lendl's firm grip on the No. 1 position.

Above Right: Swedish tennis fans show their support for their country's new star, Stefan Edberg.

Right: Boris Becker becomes the first German to reach No. 1 after winning the Australian Open.

Far Right: Jim Courier falls to Becker in the 1992 ATP World Championships, but ends the year as No. 1.

1989

Becker's rise to prominence continues, as the German captures a third Wimbledon title as well as the US Open title.

Yet Lendl finishes 10-2 in finals along with a 79-7 match record and becomes the first player to regain the year-end No. 1 ranking with an interruption in between.

1990

The ATP Tour era begins with an equal partnership between players and tournaments. The circuit features 76 tournaments in 28 countries on 6 continents.

August 13: Stefan Edberg ends Lendl's 80-week hold on No. 1 after winning the ATP Championships in Cincinnati. He becomes the third Swede (after Borg, and Wilander) to finish as year-end No. 1.

1991

January 28: One day after winning his second Australian Open title, Becker becomes the first German to hold the No. 1 ranking.

September 9: Edberg reclaims No. 1 after winning his first of two US Open crowns. He finishes No. 1 for a second year in a row.

1992

February 10: Jim Courier, at age 21 years and 5 months, becomes the 10th player (third American) to rank No. 1. Courier had opened the season with his first of two Australian Open titles, and also triumphed at Roland Garros that year.

The 1992 season also sees young American Andre Agassi break through at Grand Slam level at the most unlikely of places. Agassi, who had expressed an aversion to playing on grass early in his career, defeats Goran Ivanisevic in a five-set thriller at Wimbledon to win his first Grand Slam title.

Courier finishes as the 1992 year-end No. 1.

"Being No. 1 is iconic – there are not a lot of us around"

By Neil Harman

Pete Sampras
1993 · 1994 · 1995 · 1996 · 1997 · 1998

Pete Sampras always had the mark of a No.1. There was something in the way he moved, on the court and off it, in his quiet, implicit determination, single-mindedness, his preference for privacy and yet his love of the biggest court in the world, that marked the American as someone special.

And so it proved when he reached the position, though when it happened, when he was competing in Hong Kong, in the spring of 1993, it somehow didn't feel right. He had won the US Open as a 19-year-old two and a half years earlier, but it was not until he became the Wimbledon champion for the first of seven times, later in '93 – "I really felt I deserved it in some fashion because in the perception of a lot of people, I really was the No.1."

Sampras was not the first to concede that the vagaries of the ranking system was such

that someone could rise to this rarefied position without having won a Grand Slam and he has described it as a '**controversial ascent**' because of that. He was the most consistent player in the world but whereas his contemporary Jim Courier had won four Grand Slams and had '**taken charge of our generation**' he still had just the one in his pocket. That was to change and change decisively later that year – at Wimbledon.

"It has to be in your blood. I fought so hard for it and I wanted to keep it. It's the ultimate. There is nowhere else to go after you are the No. 1. It is a very special feeling."

The first of Sampras' seven singles victories upon the lawns of SW19 was a moment of release and refreshment, the beginning of his career as a dominant champion. "It was there that I discovered that I really wanted to be a champion, that I had a champion's heart and mind and will," he recalls. Sampras was a throwback, a player whose style was that of being the aggressor, of moving up the court as often and as stealthily as possible, a serve, a decisive volley if possible, and if a bead of sweat had formed on his brow through the excess of such a rally, he would wipe it away with the back of his thumb.

From that Wimbledon breakthrough, records tumbled including the 286 weeks he spent as the No. 1 player (a record only surpassed by Roger Federer), the accumulation of 64 titles, including 14 Grand Slams, the all-consuming desire to be the best for as long as it was possible while, at the same time, remaining a quiet, understated, rather introverted man.

"I look at players who have reached the top in their various sports and it obviously requires a lot of sacrifice," he said. "You need to be able to live a certain lifestyle that may not suit everybody, to develop a routine, to keep things as simple as possible. And once you are there, of course, there is a bullseye on your chest, there is an enormous amount of pressure and a responsibility that comes with being the No. 1 player in the world. I wanted to stay at the top as long as I could. I liked it there but it meant you had to keep winning, especially the big events and that took its toll.

"I fought really hard to stay at the top, I went through traumatic experiences (dealing with the illness and subsequent death of his first professional coach Tim Gullikson from brain cancer was the hardest of all), but I learned to cope and do a lot of that on my own because there are no team-mates, this is not a fraternity, it is the ultimate 'you get out of it what you put into it' situation."

"I was able to stay at the top for a long time and I'm very proud of that. There are only a handful who were able to stay at the top for such an extended period of time. I suppose it's iconic. There are not a lot of us around."

For Sampras, that he was the best and remained the best for as long as he did, is something to cherish and, he hopes, something to pass on to the next generation. He has two sons, Christian and Ryan and says he tries to '**drop subtle hints**' to them about the virtues of hard work, of staying on top of the job, of not letting your concentration slip – of trying to be the best you can be. "Whether it's sports or it's homework, if you give it everything, there is a chance you will be rewarded and it is as simple as that really," he says. "I don't think about it (being the No. 1) every day but every now and again I'll get that nice sensation and remind myself that I was the best and stayed the best. That is a pretty cool sensation."

Sampras with coach Tim Gullikson.

Sampras finishes the 1997 season in style, with both the ATP Tour World Championships trophy and the World No. 1 trophy to his name.

1993 Hong Kong final: Sampras captures the title in his first week at No. 1.

"Once you are there, of course, there is a bullseye on your chest, there is an enormous amount of pressure and a responsibility that comes with being the No.1 player in the world."

"It's important for me to be the best that I can, I believe that that is being No. 1"

Andre Agassi

1999

By Peter Bodo

Several players held the No. 1 ranking for longer than Agassi, some won more titles, and others showed greater consistency throughout their careers. But few of them crafted a personal saga as compelling as Agassi's, and even fewer became such shining examples of what a career in pro tennis can lead to in a person intent on making a contribution to society.

On the more mundane side, few players have had to battle the likes of Pete Sampras and Roger Federer for a share of the prizes in pro tennis, which helps explain how a player as accomplished and, ultimately, durable as Agassi finished as the year-end No. 1 for just one year (1999) - but held the top spot off and on over the course of eight full years.

Agassi completes the career Grand Slam at Roland Garros in 1999

Looking back over a career that spanned two decades (Agassi played in his first Grand Slam tournament in 1986 and his last in 2006) and featured more drama and swings of momentum than an amusement park ride, Agassi was moved to say: "Some moments it (my career) feels longer, other moments it feels like it's flown by; you can't believe you've done it all that time... Overall, you have a strong sense for the full spectrum that you've sort of travelled."

Mention the name Agassi and the two words that immediately pop to mind (perhaps after the name of his wife, Steffi Graf) are **'personal journey'**. The son of a Las Vegas casino worker who was hell-bent on making a tennis champ out of his son, Agassi had a well-documented love-hate relationship with the game, powerfully documented in his runaway best-seller autobiography, **'Open'**. Those tumultuous, conflicted feelings dated all the way back to the tender age of 13, when Agassi became a full-time scholarship **'student'** at the IMG Nick Bollettieri Tennis Academy.

Youthful rebels who scorn ambition and the repetitive, hard physical work required of an

"What makes something (like the No. 1 ranking) special is not just what you have to gain, but what you feel there is to lose."

Agassi and Sampras were to form one of the greatest tennis rivalries of all time.

aspiring pro, the way young Agassi did, rarely last long among the legions of youngsters – and parents – who would give anything to taste even modest professional success in tennis. But Agassi was different; in addition to everything else, he was nothing less than a genius.

Agassi's extraordinary talent expressed itself in a streamlined, precise game built upon a rock solid forehand and a stinging, two-handed backhand. His service return, said by some to be the best in the game – ever – was a major part of his arsenal. In that and myriad other ways, including his longevity, Agassi was much like Jimmy Connors. The game plan was as devastating as it was basic: take the ball early, with relatively flat strokes, and simply dial up the pace of the ensuing rally until your opponent makes an error, or such a weak shot that it invites a put-away.

Over those two decades, Agassi won eight Grand Slam titles and is one of just seven men in tennis history to accomplish a '**career Grand Slam**' – victory at least once in each of the four Grand Slam tournaments. He put

the final piece of that puzzle into place at Roland Garros in 1999, during the spectacular year that would help shape his legacy and remove what was left of the '**underachiever**' label attached to his name. Agassi ultimately collected 60 singles titles.

But Agassi will be just as well-remembered - and even more loved - for the way he played out the role of tennis's prodigal son. In his early, rebellious years, he was famous for his showmanship, his tradition-defying outfits (one kit featured hot pink spandex compression shorts under his black shorts, and his faux-denim '**acid washed**' shorts are ensconced safely in the fashion faux pas hall of fame), and his tendency to come up short when expectations that were great, but commensurate with his talent, were placed on him.

Agassi also had a punk-ish contempt for authority, yet even the bits that weren't welcome really energised the game and brought it out of the doldrums in which it languished in the early 1990s. "I had moments of my actions and words not reflecting who it

is I am," he has said. "If that defines a punk, then yes, absolutely that's what I was."

Agassi joined the elite rank of players almost immediately, a finalist at the French Open in 1990 and a Wimbledon champ in 1992. But by 1996 he was in the throes of personal crisis brought on partly by his increasing disenchantment with the game, and partly by a chronic wrist injury.

Agassi hit his low point in 1997, when his marriage with actress Brooke Shields was failing and his ranking plummeted to No.141. But he re-dedicated himself and rebounded the following year, setting the stage for his greatest year, 1999. From that point to the end of his career in 2006 Agassi won over sceptics and stunned critics not just with his terrific results, but by emerging as a beloved ambassador for the game.

Agassi had become reconciled to the demands and challenges of his profession with that unexpected win at Roland Garros in 1999. He describes it this way, when mulling over the process that made him the year-end No.1:

"I feel like you have to always prove that you're the best - Player of the Year, or No.1, whatever - every time you step on the court. To accomplish two Slams, which is something that nobody else did this year, makes me feel like I certainly have accomplished the most. But that's less important to me than getting on that court and getting after it every time. I really feel the pressure and the responsibility of being No.1, regardless what the situation is."

Once Agassi learned to embrace rather than repudiate his inner tennis player, he found that the respect and bully pulpit it earned for him were vital tools in the long term for creating a more meaningful life. He started the Andre Agassi College Preparatory Academy for at-risk kids in his home town of Las Vegas, and over the years he's established himself as one of the most well-respected and articulate philanthropists on the social landscape.

Like all good journeys, Agassi's has been a long one filled with unexpected stops and delightful surprises.

"I am not a normal player, I am a different kind, and one day I will be No. 1 in the world"

15-year-old Kuerten, in a postcard to his mother.

Gustavo Kuerten
2000

By Peter Bodo

Perhaps the only thing stranger than the clairvoyant moment Gustavo Kuerten experienced in the world's greatest art museum was the way his premonition came to pass. He became No. 1 for the first time, as well as No. 1 for the year, at the last possible moment - when he toppled Andre Agassi in the final match of the final event on the ATP season in 2000, the Tennis Masters Cup in Lisbon.

Oh, and on the previous day, '**Guga**' had ousted Pete Sampras. Between them, Sampras and Agassi had finished No. 1 every year since 1993. But 2000 belonged to Guga, the first and only South American so far to finish the year at the summit of the game.

Kuerten embraces his mother after winning Roland Garros in 2001.

Kuerten draws the iconic heart into the clay of the court Philippe Chatrier.

"My first time at the French Open, as a 15-year-old junior, I visited the Louvre museum. I found there this painting, and a postcard of that painting (Le Jeune Martyre, by Paul Delaroche, 1855). I sent my mother that postcard and I wrote: 'This is not a normal painting and I am not a normal player, I am a different kind, and one day I will be No. 1 in the world.' The funny thing for me is that I really didn't have those expectations in my mind – yet I wrote that. My mother still has that postcard."

Kuerten was born in Florianopolis, Brazil, in September of 1976. He experienced major tragedy long before he won a major title. His father, Aldo, died of a heart attack while umpiring a junior tennis match when Guga was just eight years old. Guga's younger brother Guilherme suffered irreparable brain damage at birth and lived a severely impaired life until he died in 2007, after accumulating the roomful of trophies that his brother Gustavo dutifully brought home.

Those **'presents'** included three replicas of the Coupe des Mousquetaires, the trophy earned by the male French Open singles champion. Kuerten won the trophy three times (1997, 2000, '01), celebrating with what would become an iconic image in tennis: Kuerten

using his racquet to draw a great big heart in the red clay of the Court Philippe Chatrier.

Unbeknownst to many, Kuerten had developed his game on a type of hard court popular during his youth in Brazil. A lean and lanky 6-foot-3, Guga had a fluid, explosive serve. He appeared in 29 finals, winning 20 titles. He was a remarkably smooth player who took long, elegant cuts at the ball – a style that worked against him on the faster surfaces so common in those days.

Kuerten was much loved for his simple and unpretentious ways. Rejecting the idea that the No. 1 ranking is a burden, he says: "You want to maintain your balance, but that's what I always tried to do. If anything, it was

Kuerten celebrates with members of his team in Lisbon, including coach Larri Passos and his mother, Alice.

Kuerten's legion of fans were ever-present on the Tour.

the opposite of a burden. It was good. I never expected it to happen to me, so I enjoyed it. What is important is to recognise that this is just a stage. One day you stop, you're not the best forever. It's wise to know that life is not always like this."

An intensely loyal man, Kuerten was 14 when he met the man who would coach him for his entire career, Larri Passos. The coach convinced Kuerten's family that Guga could succeed as a professional, and even his protégé had his doubts. "I had no ambition to be No. 1 because I couldn't imagine that far," he says. "It was too long for my expectations and my reality. Perhaps if I had grown up as a soccer player... that's normal for people in Brazil. My goal in tennis was just to be part

of the top class who played tournaments and Grand Slam events. I believe Larri was more conscious of this target, he was planning for me from the beginning."

Passos' ambitions paid off in a big way when Guga won Roland Garros at age 20 in 1997, after having played in just two previous Grand Slam events. The soundtrack to his straight-sets win over two-time French Open champion Sergi Bruguera was provided by the legion of Brazilian fans who charmed the spectators and a global television audience with their drumming, singing and dancing. It was like nothing Roland Garros habitués had ever experienced and they loved every moment of it.

Guga was in the hunt for the No. 1 ranking at various times during his career, but going into the 2000 Tennis Masters Cup in Lisbon it looked as if he would once again fall a few swings short. Marat Safin's destiny was in his own hands; he was ranked No. 1, and if he won three matches he would be guaranteed the year-end top ranking as well. Safin won two matches, but he lost to Sampras in the round robin stage and then Agassi in the semi-finals. It meant that Kuerten could wind up No. 1 – if he managed to beat the two dominant Americans on the indoor hard court that so suited their styles of play.

The trouble was, Kuerten was so banged up that he couldn't practise, focusing instead on treatment and recovery. But his pessimism

was a godsend. "I felt more comfortable with lower expectations," he remembers. "It was more similar to what I like. To enjoy it. To smile."

The rest, as they say, is history. Guga survived a three-set epic with Sampras and then played one of the best matches of his career against Agassi. Suddenly, he was No. 1. For the next day, for the entire year. Guga still savours the moment: "It was only like a dream. Impossible to imagine how much can change in five or six days. But it shows how tennis can be, how close it is. In my career there were two circumstances that cannot be explained. Roland Garros in 1997, and this special week in Lisbon."

"Getting to No. 1 is not just one event – it's the year. That's the toughest thing"

Lleyton Hewitt
2001 · 2002

By Neil Harman

Becoming the World No.1 would not lose much of its lustre if it happened when you were sitting on your sofa at home necking a cold one, but to earn such an accolade in front of your own people, winning a match in your own country against one of your own – what could be more appropriate than that?

That is the story of Lleyton Hewitt, the Australian whose accession to the position came at the Tennis Masters Cup in Sydney in 2001, when he was 20 years old playing Pat Rafter, his hero. It brought to a close the year that endorsed the credentials of the kid with attitude in the back-to-front cap who not that many years before had spent his time working as hard as he could in the backyard of his then coach Darren Cahill's home in West Lakes, an Adelaide suburb.

"It was satisfaction more than anything that the hard work and sacrifices and everything you've done from your junior career had paid off. Growing up, the three things I wanted to do were win a Grand Slam, the Davis Cup and get to World No. 1. In the end, the World No. 1 was the last of the three."

Hewitt had won the US Open in September of that year, a blistering endorsement of his young talents, taking the game audaciously to Pete Sampras in the final and in a flourish of winners, prevailing in three sets. "Going into the US Open, I was ranked four, and winning it obviously gave me an opportunity to have a crack at No. 1 for the end of the year," he said. "Making the Masters Cup in Sydney was massive as well for me. For both Pat and I, it was a goal to get in it and it was fantastic to do it alongside him."

Hewitt had worked out that, upon entering the Masters, the tussle for No. 1 was between himself Gustavo Kuerten, the colourful Brazilian and Andre Agassi, from the USA. As usual at the start of this event with its round robin element, there were countless mathematical possibilities but as it happened, Hewitt needed only to win his three qualification matches.

He defeated Sebastien Grosjean of France on the first day, Agassi two days later in straight sets and then watched as Russian Yevgeny Kafelnikov defeated Kuerten, which meant that if he beat Rafter later that night, the ultimate accolade would be his. One might have thought that prospect would unnerve him, but Hewitt reached the summit in style, a crunching 7-6, 6-2 victory over Rafter.

"It was a great feeling and pretty emotional because I was there with a great mate and Rochey (Tony Roche) was coaching Pat at the time and I obviously knew Rochey very well, so it was a fantastic atmosphere," Hewitt said.

Hewitt ended up winning the season-ending title and bore the satisfied air of a young man who had achieved much to be proud of. "Having watched my idols growing up, (Pete) Sampras, Agassi do it, that's why it meant so much," he reflected.

"An even better achievement, I think, was the following year to hold the No. 1 ranking through the whole year and win the Tennis Masters Cup [in Shanghai] when the No. 1 ranking was up for grabs again at that tournament.

"When you look back at it, it's not just one event, it's a calendar year. That's the toughest thing, with everything else that could happen. It is the hallmark of consistency and an awesome achievement once you get it.

Hewitt sees off Sampras in the 2001 US Open final.

Hewitt embraces Pat Rafter at the net following their round robin match. The win was enough to secure Hewitt the year-end No. 1 ranking.

Everyone played a different role but it was fantastic to share it with my support team at the time. Darren (Cahill) was my coach and I had worked with him since I was 14-15 years old just in his backyard in Adelaide in West Lakes. That night when I beat Pat, I remember Rochey and Pat coming up, Pat at the net and Rochey afterwards to congratulate me - it just meant a lot.

"I walked back into my locker room - everybody had their own locker room - and I had never met Greg Norman [the golfer] before and I had a message to give him a call and he was saying '**Well done mate**' just minutes after I'd won and got the No. 1 trophy."

2001 Tennis Masters Cup, Sydney: Hewitt celebrates winning the season-ending Tennis Masters Cup in his home country.

"The No. 1 ranking is something that nobody can take away"

Andy Roddick
2003

By Peter Bodo

Growing up, Andy Roddick wanted only to keep playing, to make it as a day-in, day-out working tennis pro. He never dreamed of being ranked highly, no less finishing as the No. 1 player for any given year. "When I was 15 or so I think I was just number 15 in the state of Florida. So to think of myself being No. 1 in the world as a pro, well it would have been like, 'All right, which planet are you on?'"

"I was at the Paris Masters tournament when I got the news that I made No. 1, and when I walked into the locker room the next morning a bunch of the guys walked up to me to shake my hand and say 'Well done.' And it was different from the typical, post-match handshake.

A lot of my career I wasn't even sure I was liked by a lot of guys outside the States, so to have that variety of players come up, and regardless of any personal feeling toward me, express their respect – it was unexpected, and it was just a great, great moment."

Roddick, Juan Carlos Ferrero and Roger Federer all entered the 2003 Tennis Masters Cup in a three-way race to finish the season as No.1.

One of the signature traits of Roddick is that while he could be as brash and edgy as any player who ever hefted a racquet, he sustained a fundamental humility and sense of his own good fortune until the day he retired from tennis at the 2012 US Open.

The pay-off for his lifelong habit of never resting on his laurels was the realisation of that dream he never dared to entertain; just weeks after he hit No.1 on the computer, Roddick locked up the year-end No.1 ranking as well, despite heavy pressure from two rivals – Juan Carlos Ferrero, and the rapidly improving Swiss who would take over that ranking the following year and become Roddick's career nemesis, Roger Federer.

As nemeses go, the all-time Grand Slam singles title leader isn't a bad one to have.

"I was only there for a cup of coffee," Roddick says of his year at the top. "But once you get that ranking it's something that won't ever go away, regardless of any meltdowns, or bad matches, or anything. You can get hot and win a Grand Slam over a two week period, but the year-end ranking is a 52-week process. You can look at a lot of Slam winners and the public has already forgotten them, but the year-end number ones, I think they're the ones remembered in our sport."

Roddick's unflinching analysis of his own shortcomings points toward what is probably

his greatest asset (including that behemoth serve of Roddick's): he cherished his status as an elite player, and fought a remarkably long, intense, and successful battle to keep it. "All of a sudden, early in my career, I found myself defending a runner-up finish at Wimbledon, or some other event. That part was always really foreign to me, and kind of tough. Because I knew that if I was in a semi, or a final, I was usually on the lesser end of the talent scale. The things that got me through then were a good work ethic and being mentally tough."

A Nebraska native who grew up and developed his game in Florida, Roddick won just one major - the 2003 US Open. But he was usually in the hunt for the title at every major but the

clay-court French Open. In fact, he lost to just one man in his four other trips to a Grand Slam final: Federer.

Roddick's style was unusual. The serve was his outstanding weapon but, despite his solid, 6-foot-2 frame, he was never fully comfortable attacking the net. He relied on cobbling together service breaks with a baseline game featuring a dangerous forehand and a two-handed backhand that evolved over the years from an attackable weakness into a wisely used and versatile tool.

The outstanding feature on Roddick's résumé is his consistency. He was in the Top 10 for nine years, and a Grand Slam quarter-finalist

Roddick entertains on Live! with Regis and Kelly after his 2003 US Open triumph.

Roddick poses alongside 41st US President George H. W. Bush after being presented with the No.1 trophy in Houston.

17 times. Roddick played nine Masters 1000 finals (all on hard courts), and won five. At a time when American tennis was in decline, he was a stalwart Davis Cup star, helping the US win the Cup in 2007. At 33-12, he trails only John McEnroe (41-8) as a prolific singles winner. Roddick won 32 singles titles in his 12-year career.

Roddick learned that he clinched the year-end No.1 ranking in 2003 in Houston in November, at the Tennis Masters Cup. Having played earlier in the day, he was in a Mexican restaurant with friends, hunched over and listening to the final points of Andre Agassi's match with Juan Carlos Ferrero over a telephone connected with that of a friend back at the stadium. When Agassi won it, Roddick was assured his place in tennis history.

"The coolest thing about it for me was that my childhood idol won the match that made me No.1," he remembers. "I grew up watching Pete (Sampras) and Andre. I was one of those kids in the unfortunate jean shorts-and-spandex outfit. It was amazing to see it come full circle, it was just one of those **'somebody pinch me so I know this is real'** moments. It was surreal."

There was more of the surreal to come. The following day, Roddick lost a three-set, two tie-breaker round robin match in Houston to Rainer Schuettler. But he was presented with the year-end trophy to celebrate his status as No.1 for 2003. The presenter was a prominent tennis fan - 41st US President George Herbert Walker Bush.

"The photographers wanted me to hold up my finger, to signal I was No.1 for the year," Roddick recalls. "And President Bush leaned over to me and whispered, **'After that match, I'll bet you feel like holding up a different finger.'** That's the kind of thing I remember best – the small moments, the inside joke with a former President, the little personal things that mean more to you than the obvious things that go with that ranking and honour."

It may have been, as Roddick says, just a **'cup of coffee**,' but it tasted awfully good - and its salutary effects lasted a long, long time.

1993 - 2003
In Focus

Left: Pete Sampras remained focused on the No.1 ranking throughout the 1990s.

Top Right: Marcelo Rios on his way to capturing the Miami title in 1998. The win would seal his position at No.1.

Bottom Right: Carlos Moya during his run to the Indian Wells final in 1999.

Below: Andre Agassi serves during the 1995 US Open final in which he would lose out to his long-time rival Pete Sampras.

1993

April 12: The Pete Sampras era at No.1 officially begins as the 21-year-old Californian takes over the top spot from countryman and rival Jim Courier after winning the Japan Open in Tokyo.

Sampras wins Wimbledon and the US Open that year to finish as No.1 for the first of a record six years in a row.

1994 - 97

During Sampras' dominance, the American captures 43 of his 64 career titles during a six-year stretch, including 10 (of 14) Grand Slam crowns and eight (of 11) ATP World Tour Masters 1000 titles.

Throughout his heyday, Sampras fends off stiff competition for his No.1 ranking from the likes of Michael Chang, Michael Stich and Goran Ivanisevic, all of whom come within touching distance of the top ranking, only to be thwarted by the big-serving American.

Only Agassi (who first became No.1 on April 10, 1995) and Thomas Muster (February 12, 1996) provide brief interruptions to Sampras' residency at No.1.

1998

March 30: After a run of 102 consecutive weeks at No.1 from Sampras, Chilean Marcelo Rios becomes the first South American to rank No.1 after capturing the ATP World Tour Masters 1000 title in Miami. Rios holds the top spot for a total of six weeks before Sampras reasserts himself to become a record six-time year-end No.1.

1999

The No.1 ranking changes hands between five different players, including a record three first-time No.1 players in the same season.

March 15: Carlos Moya becomes the first Spaniard at No.1 after reaching the final in Indian Wells, only to be overtaken by Yevgeny Kafelnikov on May 3.

July 26: Patrick Rafter becomes the only player to date to hold No.1 for one week only in his career.

September 13: Agassi takes over No.1 from Sampras after the Las Vegas native outlasts Todd Martin in five sets to win his second US Open title. At 29, Agassi finishes the season atop the rankings for the first time, becoming the oldest year-end No.1 since Ivan Lendl (29) in 1989. The achievement crowns a phenomenal comeback from Agassi, who had plummeted to 141 in the Emirates ATP Rankings just two years earlier.

Far Left: Gustavo Kuerten on his way to capturing his second of three Roland Garros titles.

Left Top: Marat Safin celebrates after winning the US Open in 2000.

Left Bottom: Lleyton Hewitt signs for fans during his title-winning run in Indian Wells in 2002.

Below: Andy Roddick celebrates after winning his maiden Grand Slam title at the US Open in 2003.

2000

September 11: Agassi's 52 weeks in top spot come to a close as Sampras regains No.1 after a runner-up finish at the US Open to big-hitting 20-year-old Marat Safin from Russia.

November 20: Safin takes over No.1 heading into the season-ending Tennis Masters Cup in Lisbon, only to relinquish the year-end position to Brazilian Gustavo 'Guga' Kuerten, who wins the year-end title in scintillating fashion to become the first and only South American year-end No.1 to date.

2001-02

November 19: Australian Lleyton Hewitt, at 20 years, 8 months, becomes the youngest year-end No.1 after capturing the Tennis Masters Cup on home soil in Sydney.

Hewitt holds the top spot for 75 weeks and finishes No.1 in 2002 as well.

A newly launched website, ATPtennis.com, highlights a new tournament structure. ATP Properties is formed, instigating a more commercial focus and new marketing, licensing and broadcasting opportunities.

2003

April 28: Agassi regains No.1 and, at 33, becomes the oldest player to hold the top spot.

September 8: Reigning Roland Garros champion Juan Carlos Ferrero becomes No.1 after reaching the US Open final.

Ferrero, Andy Roddick and Roger Federer head into the season-ending Tennis Masters Cup in a three-way race to finish as the year-end No.1. Despite Federer capturing the title, it's Roddick who prevails as No.1, becoming the youngest American year-end No.1 at 21 years, 2 months.

Roger Federer
2004 · 2005 · 2006 · 2007 · 2009

By Neil Harman

He was on Rod Laver Arena, wearing a red shirt, a pony-tail poked from above a white bandana, a forehand service return from Juan Carlos Ferrero landed long and Roger Federer could appreciate what it was like to be the very best. His instinct, after he had shaken hands with opponent and umpire, was to sink to his knees, but he did not stay there long. There was a final to savour.

That he did, winning the 2004 Australian Open title comprehensively, allowing the Swiss to leave Melbourne as a Grand Slam champion for the second time and World No.1 for the first. These are the moments that help mark a career - a life - and in the case of the man who has become the most successful player of any age, ones to reflect upon with a lot of pride. He remembers being the junior No.1 and thinking to himself: "Wow wouldn't it be great if I could do this in the pros, too?" His parents, rather more pragmatically, thought he should concentrate more on his studies.

"World No. 1 doesn't just come to you, you have to go and get it"

Federer celebrates reaching No. 1 for the first time after defeating Juan Carlos Ferrero in the semi-finals of the 2004 Australian Open.

"Being No. 1 is not one of those moments that happens and then you forget. It took me a lot of great performances to get there"

"It is a huge deal to have achieved the things that my heroes, people like Stefan Edberg and Pete Sampras did. It's not important for me to have done more but to have done something similar. To be a member of this list is truly humbling, and puts us all into that league where we understand each other I guess. That seems somewhat crazy but it is true."

Federer captures a record 17th Grand Slam title at Wimbledon and breaks Sampras' record for all-time weeks at No. 1.

"Roger could be the greatest tennis player of all time"

Rod Laver

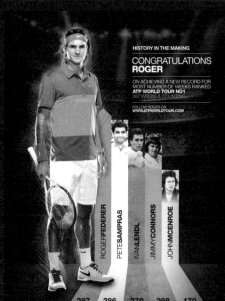

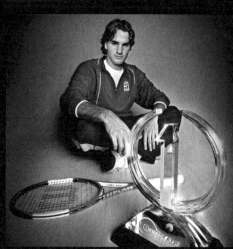

"If you want to be a tennis player, then mould yourself on Roger Federer"

John McEnroe

Federer celebrates
reaching No. 1
in Australia, 2004.

Federer, a winner of the Laureus World Sportsman
of the Year award for four consecutive years.

"They have always been very grounded, they didn't shout that their son is the best junior in town. Even when I won junior Wimbledon, I was 300 in the world, it was like **'you might be World No.1 in the juniors, but if you don't make it in the next couple of years on the tour [300 was not making it in their eyes], then perhaps you should try something else'**. I said **'okay but I really think I can make it, I think I have a chance'**. Never in my wildest dreams did I think I could win Wimbledon or become the World No.1. Things are so distant. I remember watching Martina Hingis on television and thinking that what she was doing at 16 was incredible and to consider that what I was going to achieve would be more than she had was completely unrealistic."

But reality has often been suspended where Federer is concerned. Time after time as the years have passed Federer has astounded

us with a talent that endures and a devotion to the sport and its tradition that heartens those of like mind. Records have tumbled, opponents have come and gone, he has been the benchmark for how to handle yourself and how to achieve greatness without so much as apparently shedding a bead of sweat.

"I'm not complaining. I have had much more success than I thought I would, I have been able to enjoy it in the process, it has not all been work, work, work and putting my head down and not seeing left and right and putting these things on, what are they called, blinkers. I was taking it all in, there was a year like 2005 when I was in 16 out of 17 finals and felt I was running from one event to the next and trying to manage somehow – because there is so much attention, red carpets, this and that and success and practice and everything having to be exact to the hour.

"But every other year I felt I could totally enjoy it, I had the right people around me who guided me in the right direction. I have definitely made bad decisions as well along the way but I needed those to be stronger when things got tough because there are always complications. I always say it is windy at the top, there are things that are not working out for you but when you are up there, it is how it is, it is not possible to go year in year out without any problems. Somewhere down the line you will have issues, whatever they may be, of a personal nature, coaching, your body, whatever it may be and you have to try to deal with it the best you can.

"I do remember the moment really well. I went to my knees and it was **'Oh my God I made it to World No.1'** and I have the final to play in a couple of days but please let me enjoy the moment. It was a really big deal because

I made it to No.1 in the juniors and I said **'what if?'** I had been really close to it after winning Wimbledon in 2003, in Canada I was five ranking points short and against [Andy] Roddick, I lost 7-6 in the third set and double faulted twice in the tie-break. All of these things totally played on my mind because I felt if I didn't get it then, I might never get it again. Believe it or not, I had to win the Masters Cup and reach the final of the Australian Open and that's why I always say World No.1, doesn't just come to you, you have to go and get it and that's what I did. Things can happen extremely quickly, first to try to make a break on the tour and the next thing you are fighting for No.1 in the world, it is quite surreal."

"No one remembers defeats. People remember victories"

Rafael Nadal
2008 · 2010

By Neil Harman

If there was a trophy for the longest No. 1-in-waiting, it would surely be no-contest. Rafael Nadal allowed neither his form nor his spirits to drop as Roger Federer sustained an extraordinary stranglehold on the top position, and knew his time would come one day. It did, after his quarter-final match at the ATP World Tour Masters 1000 event in Cincinnati on a sultry day in 2008.

Nadal defeated his good friend Nicolas Lapentti of Ecuador in straight sets [a dinner invitation from victor to loser was typical of Rafa's personality] and his three years of being told he was the second best was at an end. There was little more he could have done to merit his rise, for he had played one of his finest tournaments at Roland Garros, not dropping a set – and only four games to Federer in the final, following that with success on grass at Queen's Club and the matchless emotion of winning Wimbledon for the first time - "feeling better than that was impossible for me."

"It was a lot of work, a lot of years fighting for it, because I spent 2005, '06, '07 and more than half of '08 all the time as No. 2 with a lot of fantastic results and victories without having the chance to be the No. 1, so I felt like I deserved it at any moment," Nadal, said. "I was being regular all the time and had lot of points in the computer [as many as Pete Sampras when he was the No. 1 player] but Roger was amazing, almost perfect all the time.

"At the start of 2008, [Novak] Djokovic won the Australian Open and I felt like **'oh, another one is here and it's going to be very difficult to be No. 1'** I was able to play amazing tennis and it gives me a lot of personal satisfaction but

A quarter-final win over Nicolas Lapentti in Cincinnati in 2008 saw Nadal reach No. 1 for the first time.

"I play each point like my life depends on it"

Rafael Nadal

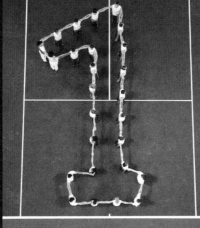

Nadal lifts the new year-end ATP World Tour No.1 trophy at the 2010 Barclays ATP World Tour Finals in London.

MADRID

The Madrid tournament celebrates Nadal's rise to No.1 in 2008.

the feeling is difficult to compare with winning a title because it is completely different. Both things you worked all your life to be there but emotions of winning a tournament for me is more amazing than being No.1 because for me, I was not more happy being No.1 than No.2. What makes me happy is being healthy and feeling I can go into every tournament and look to compete against everybody and have the chance to win. But sure I prefer to be No.1 than No.5!"

Nadal said he felt like a big player and so he was. He was thrown into the limelight as a 16-year-old, at Monte-Carlo in 2003 with a victory over the reigning Roland Garros champion Albert Costa in the second round– and he went on to become the '**King of Clay**', and an exceptional player on both grass and hard courts.

It was never part of Nadal's character to talk about the injustice of not being the best player - he appreciated what Federer meant to the sport and how remarkable it was that he sustained his form for so long – but it was an injustice he knew he wanted to put right. "Even if I am the No.1 it is just a number in

the end," the Majorcan said. "It reflects the results of one year, so when you go on court and face another player, it doesn't matter you number, you are playing someone who want to win and if you are not playing better tha your opponent, where you are in the ranking means nothing."

Some players tend to have a lull when the reach the top, they peak and they do not know what to do next – many have described it a the air going out of a balloon – but Nadal di not stop, winning the Olympic gold medal i Beijing, to give Spain another moment it woul not forget. "I was 100 per cent ready for tha week," he recalls. "I believed truly that it wa my destiny to win. And you have two perhaps three chances in a career to achieve this, s perhaps it is the hardest of all."

It would have been a terrible shame had Nada not made it to the summit. "It was something I think I deserved but [I realised it] only afte I reached it, because I didn't consider mysel that good," he said, the humble man from Manacor whose tussles with Federer becam interwoven into the sport's tapestry, a golde thread of brilliance and brutal, beautiful talent

"To be part of the group of players who I admired as a kid is something very special and means a lot. I enjoyed every moment I have been No.1 because it became a goal and I like to complete my goals and when I did it, I wanted to be there for as much time as I have the chance to be there."

"The goal for me is to be No. 1"

7-year-old Djokovic during his first TV appearance.

Novak Djokovic

2011 · 2012

By Neil Harman

Is it better to have planned for an eventuality than for it to come as a bolt from the skies? From the moment he was knee-high to a Serbian grasshopper, Novak Djokovic had it in his mind to be the best tennis player in the world. "I saw tennis on the TV and the court near my parents' restaurant, and my father brought me a small racquet," he said. "That's when we all fell in love with the sport."

It was here that Djokovic was spotted by Jelena Gencic, to whom he would return the week after his coronation to show her the trophy they had worked so hard to deliver. One thing that impressed her was how so very neatly a relative tot kept his clothes, his racquets, his equipment – he was ready for anything. "I knew that Nole would be the best in the world," she said. "Somebody asked him on the practice court: **'Hey, boy! What do you want to be when you grow up?'** [And he would reply]: 'Be the first in pro-tennis.' He was six years old."

"It is incredible to be a part of this elite, looking at the names who have ended the year as No. 1, the 16 since 1973, who have done so much for tennis on and off the court. Tennis is such a global sport but without the champions making their own mark we wouldn't be where we are now and that's something I appreciate and respect very much."

The ambition was realised across a weekend in July 2011 that he will remember with fierce pride for the rest of his life. Knowing he had completed the ascent of the rankings mountain on reaching the Wimbledon final, he went on to take Centre Court by storm, defeating Rafael Nadal to become champion for the first time and celebrate with a mouthful of the freshest grass in tennis.

"I couldn't ask for a better stage for all of my dreams to come true," Djokovic said. "From that moment, my life on the court changed because I realised that nothing is unachievable, I started to believe even more in my abilities, to gain more confidence, where I just had the feeling I can win on any surface

against anybody and that is something very important today, that positive mental mind-set that takes you to the later stages of the major events."

That year, 2011, Djokovic was in the midst of a spell touched by magic. He won his first 41 matches that year [a sequence of 43 if you include his part in the Davis Cup victory for Serbia in December 2010] on his way to seven consecutive titles. Though Roger Federer was to defeat him in the Roland Garros semi-finals, that setback served only to inspire him to greater feats at Wimbledon.

"Life creates the scenario, like a destiny and you can't fight some situations. You just try to

embrace the moment and to be thankful for being in a position to realise your childhood dream at 24. That is the thinking I've had. I was definitely very excited both positively and negatively before that Wimbledon final but being very thankful and blessed to be in that position was a big drive and helped me to prevail in that match.

"To be the youngest, newest: I try not to take it for granted. 2011 was the best year of my career and a springboard for 2012 and this year also. I am where I am today, on the practice courts each day, [because I am] surrounded by very humble people who have been with me through most of my career, helping me to stay committed and dedicated to the sport

and also to stay grounded and appreciate every single moment of what I've experienced. That's why I don't take it for granted.

"I know how much effort it takes and how many people around the world compete for that place. Being the No.1 is the pinnacle of all the ambitions of every player. Everybody wants to be the best they can be, right? That is the dream. So being in this position now, it is a marvellous feeling, I don't know how to explain it."

Djokovic has said that everything begins and ends with him. His game is based on fairly simple principles, you get the ball back into play more often than your opponents, you

wear them down by the sheer ferocity of your spirit and strategic brilliance, your body stretches itself into remarkable positions and you last longer than anyone else.

"If you cannot bring these things and manifest them on the court it doesn't make any sense having them," he said. "Tennis has become so complex in every part of life on and off the court, you need to be aware of the right people, the right lifestyle, the well-being and putting your efforts and energy into the schedule, the year and every single match you play and that is the only way in my opinion that today, you can be the No.1 in the world. I know others want to take it away and that is an extra motivation to give my best."

2004 - 2012
In Focus

Below: *Roger Federer rises to No. 1 for the first time after winning the 2004 Australian Open.*

Right: *Rafael Nadal en route to a fourth consecutive Roland Garros title in 2008.*

Far Right: *Roger Federer completes a career Grand Slam at Roland Garros in 2009, beating Sweden's Robin Soderling in the final.*

2004 - 07

February 2: Roger Federer's reign at No. 1 gets underway after the Swiss maestro wins his first Australian Open title and second overall Grand Slam crown.

Federer finishes No. 1 for the first time and his four-year dominance and record 237 consecutive weeks atop the Emirates ATP Rankings is truly underway.

During Federer's four-year perch at No. 1, he compiles an eye-popping 315-24 match record with 42 titles, including 11 of his 17 Grand Slam crowns and 13 ATP World Tour Masters 1000 titles.

In '05 he compiles an 81-4 match record and the following year he wins a personal-best 92 matches (92-5) while capturing 12 titles. In three of the four years he wins three Grand Slam titles, the only man to accomplish the feat in tennis history. From '05 Wimbledon to '07 US Open, the Swiss advances to an incredible 10 Grand Slam finals in a row.

Meanwhile, Spanish sensation Rafael Nadal establishes himself as Federer's main rival at No. 2 in the world.

2008

August 18: Having held the No. 2 ranking for a record 160 consecutive weeks, Nadal finally usurps Federer at No. 1, and finishes the season as the first left-handed No. 1 since John McEnroe in 1984.

The Mallorcan native becomes the first Spanish year-end No. 1, capturing eight titles, including Roland Garros, a first Wimbledon crown, and the Olympic gold medal.

2009

June 7: Federer captures the Roland Garros crown for the first time in his career to complete his full set of career Grand Slam titles.

July 6: Federer regains No. 1 after capturing his sixth Wimbledon title, ending Nadal's 46-week hold on No. 1.

Federer finishes the year as No. 1, becoming the first player since Lendl in 1989 to regain the year-end No. 1 ranking (after a year's interruption).

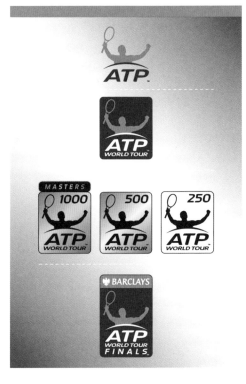

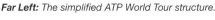

Far Left: *The simplified ATP World Tour structure.*

Left Top: *2010 US Open champion Rafael Nadal poses with the trophy in Times Square.*

Left Bottom: *Novak Djokovic celebrates as he defeats Rafael Nadal in the final of the ATP World Tour Masters 1000 event in Rome in 2011.*

Below: *Novak Djokovic holds the winner's trophy after beating Roger Federer in the final of the 2012 Barclays ATP World Tour Finals.*

2010

The ATP World Tour is unveiled with a simplified tour structure that brings a rationalised, healthier player schedule. A new points scale for rankings is implemented and tournament tiers featuring ATP World Tour Masters 1000, ATP World Tour 500 along with ATP World Tour 250 events.

2011

June 7: Nadal takes over the top spot (from Federer) after his fifth Roland Garros crown. The Spaniard adds Grand Slam titles at Wimbledon and at the US Open for the first time. He finishes No. 1 for the second time in three years.

The change at the top of the rankings leaves Federer agonisingly short of equalling Sampras' all-time weeks at No. 1, by just one week (285).

A 43-match winning streak in 2011 sees Novak Djokovic emerge as an unstoppable force as the Serb positions himself to fulfil his childhood dream of reaching the No. 1 ranking.

July 4: Djokovic fulfils his dream to become the 25th player to rank No. 1 after capturing his first Wimbledon crown.

The Serb adds his first US Open title and finishes with a 70-6 match record, highlighted by three Grand Slam titles and a season record five ATP World Tour Masters 1000 titles.

2012

July 9: Federer regains No. 1 (after a two-year absence) with his 17th Grand Slam title at Wimbledon. The win enables the Swiss to overtake Sampras for most-weeks at No. 1 (287). Federer holds the top spot for 17 weeks taking his total weeks at No. 1 to a record 302 weeks.

Andy Murray wins his first career major at the US Open to end Britain's 76-year wait for a men's singles Grand Slam champion. Murray also wins the Olympic gold medal on home soil at the All England Club.

November 5: Djokovic takes over top spot heading into the season-ending Barclays ATP World Tour Finals, in which he defeats Federer in the final to further cement his position at the top of world tennis.

No. 1 Players
1973 - 2012

With the Emirates ATP Rankings operating on a 52-week basis, achieving No. 1 status at any point in the year represents a career - defining moment - a reflection of unrivalled excellence over the previous 12 months.

In addition to the 16 year-end No. 1 players, nine other players have scaled summit of world tennis over the past 40 years.

John Newcombe

8 weeks at No. 1 - 1974

32 Career Titles in Open Era

John Newcombe, owner of arguably the most famous moustache in tennis, rounded out a 20-year golden age of Australian tennis that featured the likes of Sedgman, Hoad, Fraser, Laver, Rosewall and Emerson. With the Emirates ATP Rankings established in 1973, it was the charismatic showman known for his physicality and unshakeable self-belief who became the first Australian (and second player overall behind Nastase) to become the official World No. 1. He won seven singles and 12 doubles majors, and spent eight weeks at No. 1 in 1974 before Jimmy Connors began his 160-week streak in top spot.

"When I did become No. 1 it was a great honour and one I respect even more today"

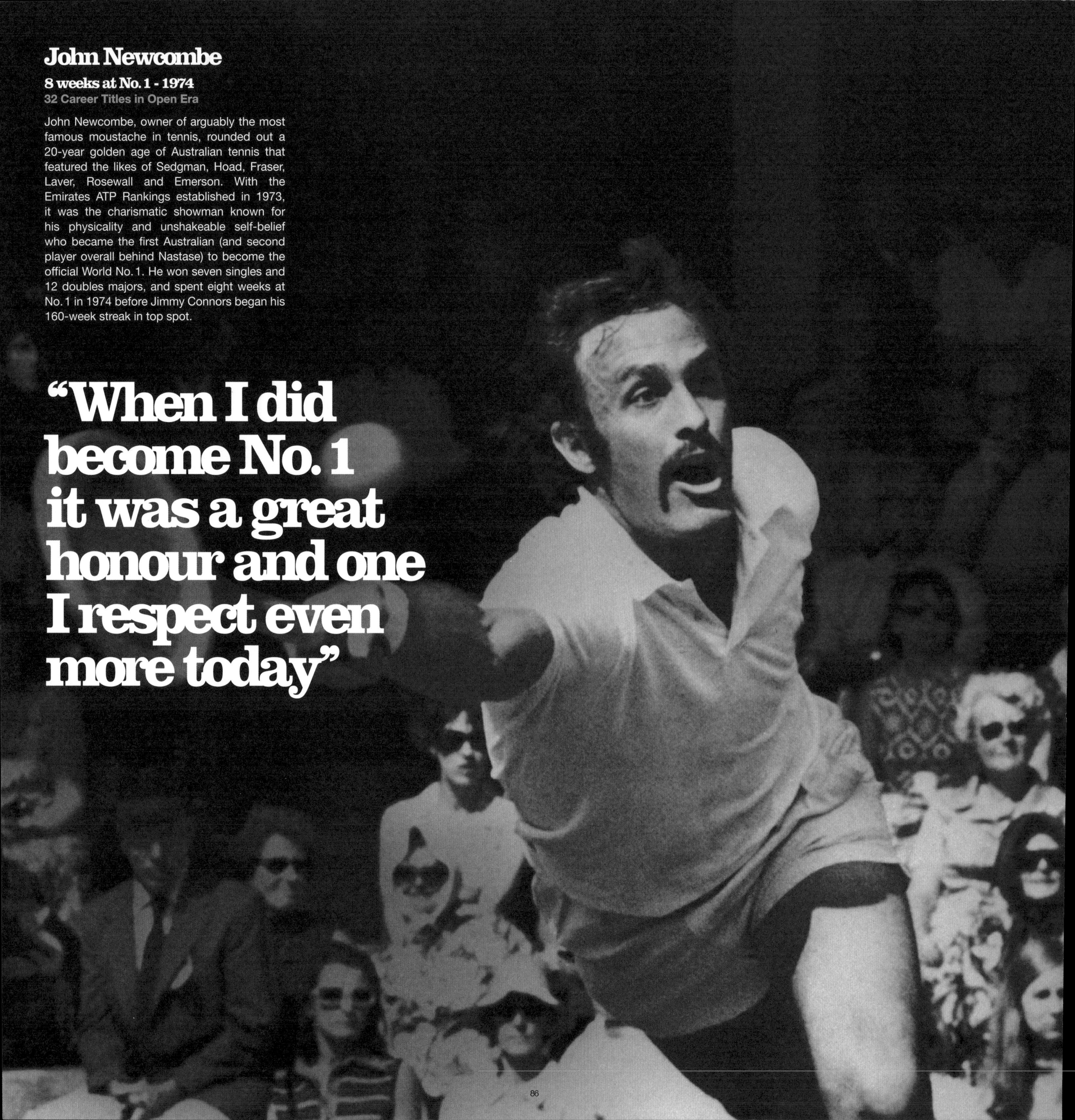

Boris Becker

12 weeks at No. 1 - 1991
49 Career Titles

Boris Becker, the explosive serve and volleyer who rocketed to fame by winning the first of his three Wimbledon titles as a 17-year-old, was one of the most famous athletes of his day. Known for his booming serve, big forehand and diving acrobatics at the net, Becker counted six majors and three year-end championships (from eight finals) among his 49 career titles. He won 713 career matches and spent 12 weeks at No. 1 in 1991.

"I can't believe it. I have to sleep on it many nights to realise that I'm [No. 1]"

Thomas Muster

6 weeks at No. 1 - 1996
44 Career Titles

After Vilas and before Nadal, the super-fit, fiercely competitive and determined Austrian was the undisputed '**King of Clay**', winning 40 of his 44 career titles on the surface, including Roland Garros in 1995 and three ATP World Tour Masters 1000s in both Monte-Carlo and Rome. The left hander spent six weeks at No. 1 in 1996. In 1989 on the eve of the Miami final, Muster was hit by a drunk driver and suffered a severe knee injury. Showing his indomitable spirit, Muster began his comeback by practising in a specially designed chair and was back on tour in six months.

"I have been dreaming about becoming No. 1 and now it's a reality"

Marcelo Rios

6 weeks at No. 1 - 1998
18 Career Titles

The sublimely talented, pony-tailed lefty will always be remembered as one of the most gifted players on tour. The only World No. 1 to never win a Grand Slam title, and the only No. 1 to hail from Chile, the 5' 9" 160-pound Rios spent six weeks at No. 1 in 1998. During his banner season, when he finished runner-up to Petr Korda at the Australian Open, Rios won three ATP World Tour Masters 1000 titles - at Indian Wells, Miami and Rome - and four other titles.

"I feel really proud being the only Chilean to become No. 1 in the world"

Carlos Moya

2 weeks at No. 1 - 1999
20 Career Titles

Tall and dashing, the bandana-clad Moya became the first Spaniard to become World No. 1 when he held top spot for two weeks in 1999 after a runner-up finish in Indian Wells. Although 16 of his 20 career titles came on clay, Moya showed he was an accomplished hard court player by winning four titles (including Cincinnati) and reaching 12 other finals, including the '97 Australian Open, on the surface. Moya won 575 career matches. Hailing from Mallorca, Moya was an instrumental mentor to Rafael Nadal.

"At least for this week I'm going to be King of the World"

Yevgeny Kafelnikov

6 weeks at No. 1 - 1999
26 Career Titles

The Russian workhorse was known for both the quality and quantity of his output during his career, three times playing more than 100 singles matches in a season. He is the last player to win 25 or more titles in both singles and doubles and in 1996 claimed a winning double at Roland Garros. No player has come close to repeating that effort since. The 2000 Olympic gold medalist also won the Australian Open in 1999, the year he spent six weeks at No.1. He won five consecutive Kremlin Cup titles between 1997-2001 on home soil in Russia. Kafelnikov won 609 singles and 358 doubles matches during his career.

"Being No. 1 was something special and was the pinnacle in my career"

"No. 1 for one week; the title that no one can take off me and no one can beat"

Patrick Rafter

1 week at No. 1 - 1999

11 Career Titles

Arguably the best serve & volleyer since Stefan Edberg, Pat Rafter was universally admired by fans for the variety he injected into an era dominated by baseliners, his unfailing sportsmanship and humility. After winning the 1997 US Open, Rafter was labelled a '**One Slam Wonder**' and responded the following year by winning back-to-back ATP World Tour Masters 1000 titles in Toronto and Cincinnati before defending his title at Flushing Meadows. Rafter, who spent just one week at No. 1 in 1999, won enthralling five-setters against Andre Agassi in 2000 and 2001 to reach two Wimbledon finals, narrowly losing the '01 final 9-7 in the fifth to Goran Ivanisevic.

"My goal is to win a Slam and be No. 1. We live because of dreams"

Marat Safin

9 weeks at No. 1 - 2000-01
15 Career Titles

Described by some as a tortured genius, popular and talented Russian Marat Safin was among the hardest ball strikers of his era and a flamboyant and charismatic personality known for his dry wit. In 2000, Safin stunned Pete Sampras in straight sets in the US Open final and later that year became, at the time, the youngest No. 1 in ATP history at 20 years and 9 months. He spent nine weeks at No. 1 and won the Australian Open in 2005, but his career haul of 15 titles arguably did not do justice to his immense talents.

Juan Carlos Ferrero

8 weeks at No. 1 - 2003
16 Career Titles

Known as 'The Mosquito,' the diminutive Spaniard was one of the best clay-court players of his generation, winning Roland Garros and three ATP World Tour Masters 1000s on the surface. But he also reached the final of the Tennis Masters Cup on indoor hard court in Shanghai in 2002, and the following season rose to No. 1 for eight weeks following a runner-up finish to Andy Roddick at the US Open. Ferrero won 479 matches in his career and claimed 16 titles (13 on clay) from 34 finals.

"It's the dream of any player and achieving it is like a dream come true"

"Not everyone can be No. 1"

Arthur Ashe

The Stats & Numbers

Over the past 40 years, 25 players have reached the summit of world tennis, with only 16 of those achieving year-end No. 1 status. But who has spent the most overall weeks at No. 1? Who was the youngest, and who was the oldest? Which players reached No. 1 in both singles and doubles? The Stats & Numbers tell you everything you need to know about the No. 1 ranking over the past 40 years.

What it takes to be
Year-End ATP World Tour No.1

There is nothing average about a year-end **ATP World Tour No.1**.

But as the chart below shows, a year-end No.1 is on average **24** years old, has played **85** matches and won **87%** of them. He has also captured **8.4** titles, of which **1.6** were Masters 1000s and **1.7** were Grand Slams.

No wonder it is arguably considered to be the **ultimate sporting achievement.**

ATP™ WORLD TOUR No.1
PRESENTED BY
Emirates

	1973	1974	1975	1976	1977	1978	1979	1980	1981	1982	1983	1984	1985	1986	1987	1988	1989	1990	1991	1992	1993
PLAYER'S AGE	27	22	23	24	25	26	23	24	22	23	24	25	25	26	27	24	29	24	25	22	22

MATCHES PLAYED: Won & Lost

Year	Matches Won	Won	Loss
1973	87.5%	119	17
1974	96%	95	4
1975	91.1%	82	8
1976	91.3%	94	9
1977	86.1%	68	11
1978	91.7%	66	6
1979	93.3%	84	6
1980	92.1%	70	6
1981	88.4%	76	10
1982	88.8%	71	9
1983	85.1%	63	11
1984	96.5%	82	3
1985	92.3%	84	7
1986	92.5%	74	6
1987	91.4%	74	7
1988	82.8%	53	11
1989	91.9%	79	7
1990	82.4%	70	15
1991	81.7%	76	17
1992	79.3%	69	18
1993	84.2%	85	16

OVERALL TITLES WON

GRAND SLAM TITLES

ILIE NASTASE	1973
JIMMY CONNORS	1974–1978
BJORN BORG	1979–1980
JOHN MCENROE	1981–1984
IVAN LENDL	1985–1987
MATS WILANDER	1988
IVAN LENDL	1989
STEFAN EDBERG	1990–1991
JIM COURIER	1992
PETE SAMPRAS	1993

98

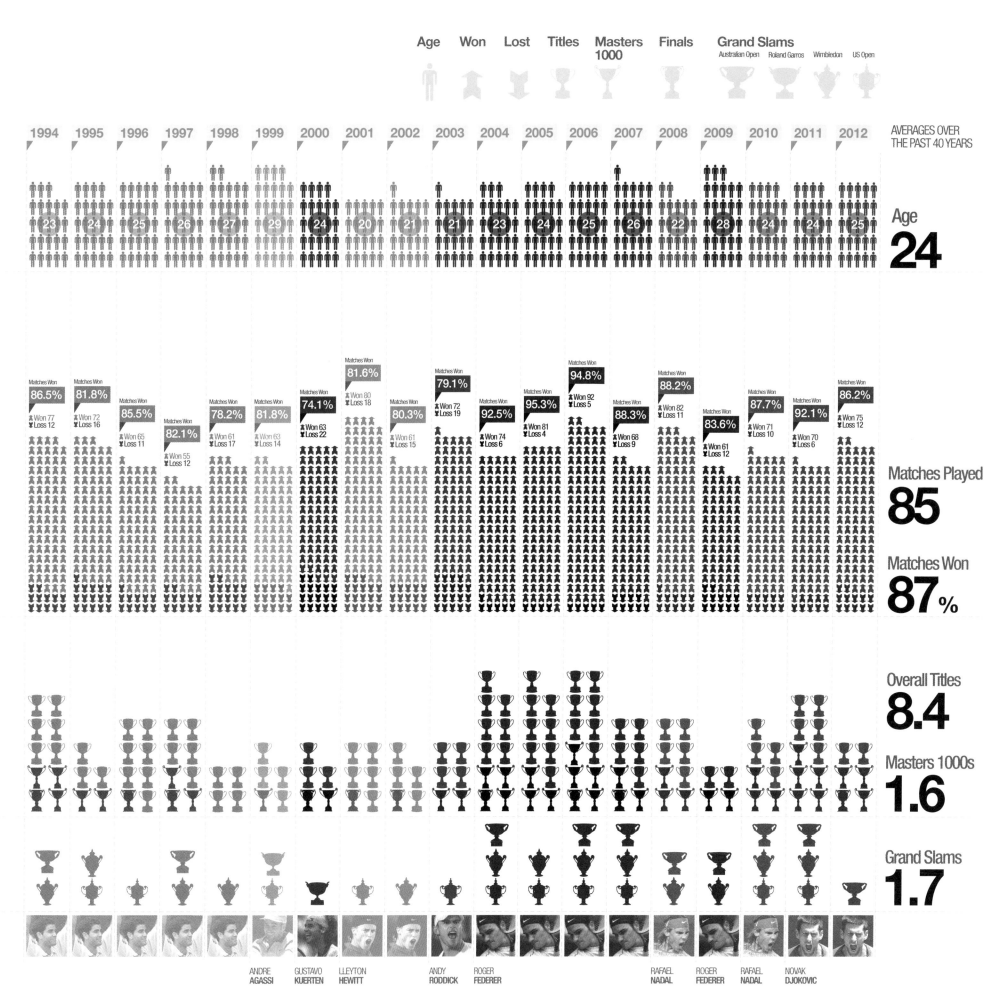

Age · Won · Lost · Titles · Masters 1000 · Finals · Grand Slams (Australian Open · Roland Garros · Wimbledon · US Open)

| 1994 | 1995 | 1996 | 1997 | 1998 | 1999 | 2000 | 2001 | 2002 | 2003 | 2004 | 2005 | 2006 | 2007 | 2008 | 2009 | 2010 | 2011 | 2012 | AVERAGES OVER THE PAST 40 YEARS |

Age
23 · 24 · 25 · 26 · 27 · 29 · 24 · 20 · 21 · 21 · 23 · 24 · 25 · 26 · 22 · 28 · 24 · 24 · 25

Age **24**

Matches Won
- 1994: 86.5% — Won 77, Loss 12
- 1995: 81.8% — Won 72, Loss 16
- 1996: 85.5% — Won 65, Loss 11
- 1997: 82.1% — Won 55, Loss 12
- 1998: 78.2% — Won 61, Loss 17
- 1999: 81.8% — Won 63, Loss 14
- 2000: 74.1% — Won 63, Loss 22
- 2001: 81.6% — Won 80, Loss 18
- 2002: 80.3% — Won 61, Loss 15
- 2003: 79.1% — Won 72, Loss 19
- 2004: 92.5% — Won 74, Loss 6
- 2005: 95.3% — Won 81, Loss 4
- 2006: 94.8% — Won 92, Loss 5
- 2007: 88.3% — Won 68, Loss 9
- 2008: 88.2% — Won 82, Loss 11
- 2009: 83.6% — Won 61, Loss 12
- 2010: 87.7% — Won 71, Loss 10
- 2011: 92.1% — Won 70, Loss 6
- 2012: 86.2% — Won 75, Loss 12

Matches Played **85**

Matches Won **87%**

Overall Titles **8.4**

Masters 1000s **1.6**

Grand Slams **1.7**

ANDRE AGASSI · GUSTAVO KUERTEN · LLEYTON HEWITT · ANDY RODDICK · ROGER FEDERER · RAFAEL NADAL · ROGER FEDERER · RAFAEL NADAL · NOVAK DJOKOVIC

Emirates ATP Rankings
History of ATP World Tour No. 1

The **Emirates ATP Rankings** operate on a 52-week rolling system that is used for entries and seedings into tournaments throughout the season. The statistics below highlight the achievements of the world's best players over the past 40 years.

ATP WORLD TOUR No.1
PRESENTED BY Emirates

Since Ilie Nastase became the first **No.1** on August 23, 1973, there have been 91 changes at the top, with 25 players holding the **No.1** ranking.

WEEKS AT NO.1

1. Ilie Nastase
Date	Weeks
Aug. 23, 1973	40

2. John Newcombe
Date	Weeks
June 3, 1974	8

3. Jimmy Connors
Date	Weeks
July 29, 1974	160
Aug. 30, 1977	84
May 21, 1979	7
Sept. 13, 1982	7
Nov. 8, 1982	1
Jan. 31, 1983	1
Feb. 14, 1983	2
May 16, 1983	3
June 13, 1983	3

4. Bjorn Borg
Date	Weeks
Aug. 23, 1977	1
Apr. 9, 1979	6
July 9, 1979	34
Mar. 24, 1980	20
Aug. 18, 1980	46
July 20, 1981	2

5. John McEnroe
Date	Weeks
Mar. 3, 1980	3
Aug. 11, 1980	1
July 6, 1981	2
Aug. 3, 1981	58
Nov. 1, 1982	1
Nov. 15, 1982	11
Feb. 7, 1983	1
June 6, 1983	1
July 4, 1983	17
Dec. 12, 1983	4
Mar. 12, 1984	13
June 18, 1984	3
Aug. 13, 1984	53
Aug. 26, 1985	2

6. Ivan Lendl
Date	Weeks
Feb. 28, 1983	11
Oct. 31, 1983	6
Jan. 9, 1984	9
June 11, 1984	1
July 9, 1984	5
Aug. 19, 1985	1
Sept. 9, 1985	157
Jan. 30, 1989	80

7. Mats Wilander
Date	Weeks
Sept. 12, 1988	20

8. Stefan Edberg
Date	Weeks
Aug. 13, 1990	24
Feb. 18, 1991	20
Sept. 9, 1991	22
Mar. 23, 1992	3
Sept. 14, 1992	3

9. Boris Becker
Date	Weeks
Jan. 28, 1991	3
July 8, 1991	9

10. Jim Courier
Date	Weeks
Feb. 10, 1992	6
Apr. 13, 1992	22
Oct. 5, 1992	27
Aug. 23, 1993	3

11. Pete Sampras
Date	Weeks
Apr. 12, 1993	19
Sept. 13, 1993	82
Nov. 6, 1995	12
Feb. 19, 1996	3
Apr. 15, 1996	102
Apr. 27, 1998	15
Aug. 24, 1998	20
Mar. 29, 1999	5
June 14, 1999	3
Aug. 2, 1999	6
Sept. 11, 2000	10

12. Andre Agassi
Date	Weeks
Apr. 10, 1995	30
Jan. 29, 1996	2
July 5, 1999	3
Sept. 13, 1999	52
Apr. 28, 2003	2
June 16, 2003	12

13. Thomas Muster
Date	Weeks
Feb. 12, 1996	1
Mar. 11, 1996	5

14. Marcelo Rios
Date	Weeks
Mar. 30, 1998	4
Aug. 10, 1998	2

15. Carlos Moya
Date	Weeks
Mar. 15, 1999	2

16. Yevgeny Kafelnikov
Date	Weeks
May 3, 1999	6

17. Patrick Rafter
Date	Weeks
July 26, 1999	1

18. Marat Safin
Date	Weeks
Nov. 20, 2000	2
Jan. 29, 2001	4
Apr. 2, 2001	3

19. Gustavo Kuerten
Date	Weeks
Dec. 4, 2000	8
Feb. 26, 2001	5
Apr. 22, 2001	30

20. Lleyton Hewitt
Date	Weeks
Nov. 19, 2001	75
May 12, 2003	5

21. Juan Carlos Ferrero
Date	Weeks
Sept. 8, 2003	8

22. Andy Roddick
Date	Weeks
Nov. 3, 2003	13

23. Roger Federer
Date	Weeks
Feb. 2, 2004	237
July 6, 2009	48
July 9, 2012	17

24. Rafael Nadal
Date	Weeks
Aug. 18, 2008	46
June 7, 2010	56

25. Novak Djokovic
Date	Weeks
July 4, 2011	53
Nov. 5, 2012	31*

*as of June 3, 2013

Total Weeks at No. 1

Player	Weeks at No.1
Roger Federer (SUI)	302
Pete Sampras (USA)	286
Ivan Lendl (CZE)	270
Jimmy Connors (USA)	268
John McEnroe (USA)	170
Bjorn Borg (SWE)	109
Rafael Nadal (ESP)	102
Andre Agassi (USA)	101
Novak Djokovic (SRB)	*84
Lleyton Hewitt (AUS)	80
Stefan Edberg (SWE)	72
Jim Courier (USA)	58
Gustavo Kuerten (BRA)	43
Ilie Nastase (ROM)	40
Mats Wilander (SWE)	20
Andy Roddick (USA)	13
Boris Becker (GER)	12
Marat Safin (RUS)	9
Juan Carlos Ferrero (ESP)	8
John Newcombe (AUS)	8
Yevgeny Kafelnikov (RUS)	6
Thomas Muster (AUT)	6
Marcelo Rios (CHI)	6
Carlos Moya (ESP)	2
Patrick Rafter (AUS)	1

*as of June 3, 2013

Age When reaching No. 1

Player	Date	Age
Lleyton Hewitt	Nov.19, 2001	20y8m
Marat Safin	Nov. 20, 2000	20y9m
John McEnroe	Mar. 3, 1980	21y15d
Andy Roddick **	Nov. 3, 2003	21y2m
Bjorn Borg	Aug. 23, 1977	21y2m
Jim Courier	Feb. 10, 1992	21y5m
Pete Sampras	Apr. 12, 1993	21y8m
Jimmy Connors	July 29, 1974	21y11m
Rafael Nadal	Aug. 18, 2008	22y2m
Marcelo Rios	Mar. 30, 1998	22y3m
Roger Federer	Feb. 2, 2004	22y5m
Carlos Moya	Mar. 15, 1999	22y6m
Ivan Lendl	Feb. 28, 1983	22y11m
Boris Becker	Jan. 28, 1991	23y2m
Juan Carlos Ferrero	Sept. 8, 2003	23y6m
Novak Djokovic	July 4, 2011	24y1m
Mats Wilander	Sept. 12, 1988	24y1m
Gustavo Kuerten	Dec. 4, 2000	24y2m
Stefan Edberg	Aug. 13, 1990	24y9m
Andre Agassi	Apr. 10, 1995	24y11m
Yevgeny Kafelnikov	May 3, 1999	25y2m
Patrick Rafter	July 26, 1999	26y8m
Ilie Nastase	Aug. 23, 1973	27y1m
Thomas Muster	Feb. 12, 1996	28y4m
John Newcombe	June 3, 1974	30y11m

Red denotes active player

** Roddick was younger than Borg when reaching No.1

Emirates ATP Rankings
History of Year-End Top 10 Singles

2012
1. Novak Djokovic (SRB)
2. Roger Federer (SUI)
3. Andy Murray (GBR)
4. Rafael Nadal (ESP)
5. David Ferrer (ESP)
6. Tomas Berdych (CZE)
7. Juan Martin del Potro (ARG)
8. Jo-Wilfried Tsonga (FRA)
9. Janko Tipsarevic (SRB)
10. Richard Gasquet (FRA)

2011
1. Novak Djokovic (SRB)
2. Rafael Nadal (ESP)
3. Roger Federer (SUI)
4. Andy Murray (GBR)
5. David Ferrer (ESP)
6. Jo-Wilfried Tsonga (FRA)
7. Tomas Berdych (CZE)
8. Mardy Fish (USA)
9. Janko Tipsarevic (SRB)
10. Nicolas Almagro (ESP)

2010
1. Rafael Nadal (ESP)
2. Roger Federer (SUI)
3. Novak Djokovic (SRB)
4. Andy Murray (GBR)
5. Robin Soderling (SWE)
6. Tomas Berdych (CZE)
7. David Ferrer (ESP)
8. Andy Roddick (USA)
9. Fernando Verdasco (ESP)
10. Mikhail Youzhny (RUS)

2009
1. Roger Federer (SUI)
2. Rafael Nadal (ESP)
3. Novak Djokovic (SRB)
4. Andy Murray (GBR)
5. Juan Martin del Potro (ARG)
6. Nikolay Davydenko (RUS)
7. Andy Roddick (USA)
8. Robin Soderling (SWE)
9. Fernando Verdasco (ESP)
10. Jo-Wilfried Tsonga (FRA)

2008
1. Rafael Nadal (ESP)
2. Roger Federer (SUI)
3. Novak Djokovic (SRB)
4. Andy Murray (GBR)
5. Nikolay Davydenko (RUS)
6. Jo-Wilfried Tsonga (FRA)
7. Andy Roddick (USA)
8. Robin Soderling (SWE)
9. Fernando Verdasco (ESP)
10. James Blake (USA)

2007
1. Roger Federer (SUI)
2. Rafael Nadal (ESP)
3. Novak Djokovic (SRB)
4. Nikolay Davydenko (RUS)
5. David Ferrer (ESP)
6. Andy Roddick (USA)
7. Fernando Gonzalez (CHI)
8. Richard Gasquet (FRA)
9. David Nalbandian (ARG)
10. Tommy Robredo (ESP)

2006
1. Roger Federer (SUI)
2. Rafael Nadal (ESP)
3. Nikolay Davydenko (RUS)
4. James Blake (USA)
5. Ivan Ljubicic (CRO)
6. Andy Roddick (USA)
7. Tommy Robredo (ESP)
8. David Nalbandian (ARG)
9. Mario Ancic (CRO)
10. Fernando Gonzalez (CHI)

2005
1. Roger Federer (SUI)
2. Rafael Nadal (ESP)
3. Andy Roddick (USA)
4. Lleyton Hewitt (AUS)
5. Nikolay Davydenko (RUS)
6. David Nalbandian (ARG)
7. Andre Agassi (USA)
8. Guillermo Coria (ARG)
9. Ivan Ljubicic (CRO)
10. Gaston Gaudio (ARG)

2004
1. Roger Federer (SUI)
2. Andy Roddick (USA)
3. Lleyton Hewitt (AUS)
4. Marat Safin (RUS)
5. Carlos Moya (ESP)
6. Tim Henman (GBR)
7. Guillermo Coria (ARG)
8. Andre Agassi (USA)
9. David Nalbandian (ARG)
10. Gaston Gaudio (ARG)

2003
1. Andy Roddick (USA)
2. Roger Federer (SUI)
3. Juan Carlos Ferrero (ESP)
4. Andre Agassi (USA)
5. Guillermo Coria (ARG)
6. Rainer Schuettler (GER)
7. Carlos Moya (ESP)
8. David Nalbandian (ARG)
9. Mark Philippoussis (AUS)
10. Sebastien Grosjean (FRA)

2002
1. Lleyton Hewitt (AUS)
2. Andre Agassi (USA)
3. Marat Safin (RUS)
4. Juan Carlos Ferrero (ESP)
5. Carlos Moya (ESP)
6. Roger Federer (SUI)
7. Jiri Novak (CZE)
8. Tim Henman (GBR)
9. Albert Costa (ESP)
10. Andy Roddick (USA)

2001
1. Lleyton Hewitt (AUS)
2. Gustavo Kuerten (BRA)
3. Andre Agassi (USA)
4. Yevgeny Kafelnikov (RUS)
5. Juan Carlos Ferrero (ESP)
6. Sebastien Grosjean (FRA)
7. Patrick Rafter (AUS)
8. Tommy Haas (GER)
9. Tim Henman (GBR)
10. Pete Sampras (USA)

2000
1. Gustavo Kuerten (BRA)
2. Marat Safin (RUS)
3. Pete Sampras (USA)
4. Magnus Norman (SWE)
5. Yevgeny Kafelnikov (RUS)
6. Andre Agassi (USA)
7. Lleyton Hewitt (AUS)
8. Alex Corretja (ESP)
9. Thomas Enqvist (SWE)
10. Tim Henman (GBR)

1999
1. Andre Agassi (USA)
2. Yevgeny Kafelnikov (RUS)
3. Pete Sampras (USA)
4. Thomas Enqvist (SWE)
5. Gustavo Kuerten (BRA)
6. Nicolas Kiefer (GER)
7. Todd Martin (USA)
8. Nicolas Lapentti (ECU)
9. Marcelo Rios (CHI)
10. Richard Krajicek (NED)

1998
1. Pete Sampras (USA)
2. Marcelo Rios (CHI)
3. Alex Corretja (ESP)
4. Patrick Rafter (AUS)
5. Carlos Moya (ESP)
6. Andre Agassi (USA)
7. Tim Henman (GBR)
8. Karol Kucera (SVK)
9. Greg Rusedski (GBR)
10. Richard Krajicek (NED)

1997
1. Pete Sampras (USA)
2. Patrick Rafter (AUS)
3. Michael Chang (USA)
4. Jonas Bjorkman (SWE)
5. Yevgeny Kafelnikov (RUS)
6. Greg Rusedski (GBR)
7. Carlos Moya (ESP)
8. Sergi Bruguera (ESP)
9. Thomas Muster (AUT)
10. Marcelo Rios (CHI)

1996
1. Pete Sampras (USA)
2. Michael Chang (USA)
3. Yevgeny Kafelnikov (RUS)
4. Goran Ivanisevic (CRO)
5. Thomas Muster (AUT)
6. Boris Becker (GER)
7. Richard Krajicek (NED)
8. Andre Agassi (USA)
9. Thomas Enqvist (SWE)
10. Wayne Ferreira (RSA)

1995
1. Pete Sampras (USA)
2. Andre Agassi (USA)
3. Thomas Muster (AUT)
4. Boris Becker (GER)
5. Michael Chang (USA)
6. Yevgeny Kafelnikov (RUS)
7. Thomas Enqvist (SWE)
8. Jim Courier (USA)
9. Wayne Ferreira (RSA)
10. Goran Ivanisevic (CRO)

1994
1. Pete Sampras (USA)
2. Andre Agassi (USA)
3. Boris Becker (GER)
4. Sergi Bruguera (ESP)
5. Goran Ivanisevic (CRO)
6. Michael Chang (USA)
7. Stefan Edberg (SWE)
8. Alberto Berasategui (ESP)
9. Michael Stich (GER)
10. Todd Martin (USA)

1993
1. Pete Sampras (USA)
2. Michael Stich (GER)
3. Jim Courier (USA)
4. Sergi Bruguera (ESP)
5. Stefan Edberg (SWE)
6. Andrei Medvedev (UKR)
7. Goran Ivanisevic (CRO)
8. Michael Chang (USA)
9. Thomas Muster (AUT)
10. Cedric Pioline (FRA)

1992
1. Jim Courier (USA)
2. Stefan Edberg (SWE)
3. Pete Sampras (USA)
4. Goran Ivanisevic (CRO)
5. Boris Becker (GER)
6. Michael Chang (USA)
7. Petr Korda (CZE)
8. Ivan Lendl (USA)
9. Andre Agassi (USA)
10. Richard Krajicek (NED)

1991
1. Stefan Edberg (SWE)
2. Jim Courier (USA)
3. Boris Becker (GER)
4. Michael Stich (GER)
5. Ivan Lendl (CZE)
6. Pete Sampras (USA)
7. Guy Forget (FRA)
8. Karel Novacek (CZE)
9. Petr Korda (CZE)
10. Andre Agassi (USA)

1990
1. Stefan Edberg (SWE)
2. Boris Becker (GER)
3. Ivan Lendl (CZE)
4. Andre Agassi (USA)
5. Pete Sampras (USA)
6. Andres Gomez (ECU)
7. Thomas Muster (AUT)
8. Emilio Sanchez (ESP)
9. Goran Ivanisevic (CRO)
10. Brad Gilbert (USA)

1989
1. Ivan Lendl (CZE)
2. Boris Becker (GER)
3. Stefan Edberg (SWE)
4. John McEnroe (USA)
5. Michael Chang (USA)
6. Brad Gilbert (USA)
7. Andre Agassi (USA)
8. Aaron Krickstein (USA)
9. Alberto Mancini (ARG)
10. Jay Berger (USA)

1988
1. Mats Wilander (SWE)
2. Ivan Lendl (CZE)
3. Andre Agassi (USA)
4. Boris Becker (GER)
5. Stefan Edberg (SWE)
6. Kent Carlsson (SWE)
7. Jimmy Connors (USA)
8. Jakob Hlasek (SUI)
9. Henri Leconte (FRA)
10. Tim Mayotte (USA)

1987
1. Ivan Lendl (CZE)
2. Stefan Edberg (SWE)
3. Mats Wilander (SWE)
4. Jimmy Connors (USA)
5. Boris Becker (GER)
6. Miloslav Mecir (CZE)
7. Pat Cash (AUS)
8. Yannick Noah (FRA)
9. Tim Mayotte (USA)
10. John McEnroe (USA)

1986
1. Ivan Lendl (CZE)
2. Boris Becker (GER)
3. Mats Wilander (SWE)
4. Yannick Noah (FRA)
5. Stefan Edberg (SWE)
6. Henri Leconte (FRA)
7. Joakim Nystrom (SWE)
8. Jimmy Connors (USA)
9. Miloslav Mecir (CZE)
10. Andres Gomez (ECU)

1985
1. Ivan Lendl (CZE)
2. John McEnroe (USA)
3. Mats Wilander (SWE)
4. Jimmy Connors (USA)
5. Stefan Edberg (SWE)
6. Boris Becker (GER)
7. Yannick Noah (FRA)
8. Anders Jarryd (SWE)
9. Miloslav Mecir (CZE)
10. Kevin Curren (USA)

1984
1. John McEnroe (USA)
2. Jimmy Connors (USA)
3. Ivan Lendl (CZE)
4. Mats Wilander (SWE)
5. Andres Gomez (ECU)
6. Anders Jarryd (SWE)
7. Henrik Sundstrom (SWE)
8. Pat Cash (AUS)
9. Eliot Teltscher (USA)
10. Yannick Noah (FRA)

1983
1. John McEnroe (USA)
2. Ivan Lendl (CZE)
3. Jimmy Connors (USA)
4. Mats Wilander (SWE)
5. Yannick Noah (FRA)
6. Jimmy Arias (USA)
7. Jose Higueras (ESP)
8. Jose-Luis Clerc (ARG)
9. Kevin Curren (RSA)
10. Gene Mayer (USA)

1982
1. John McEnroe (USA)
2. Jimmy Connors (USA)
3. Ivan Lendl (CZE)
4. Guillermo Vilas (ARG)
5. Vitas Gerulaitis (USA)
6. Jose-Luis Clerc (ARG)
7. Mats Wilander (SWE)
8. Gene Mayer (USA)
9. Yannick Noah (FRA)
10. Peter McNamara (AUS)

1981
1. John McEnroe (USA)
2. Ivan Lendl (CZE)
3. Jimmy Connors (USA)
4. Bjorn Borg (SWE)
5. Jose-Luis Clerc (ARG)
6. Guillermo Vilas (ARG)
7. Gene Mayer (USA)
8. Eliot Teltscher (USA)
9. Vitas Gerulaitis (USA)
10. Peter McNamara (AUS)

1980
1. Bjorn Borg (SWE)
2. John McEnroe (USA)
3. Jimmy Connors (USA)
4. Gene Mayer (USA)
5. Guillermo Vilas (ARG)
6. Ivan Lendl (CZE)
7. Harold Solomon (USA)
8. Jose-Luis Clerc (ARG)
9. Vitas Gerulaitis (USA)
10. Eliot Teltscher (USA)

1979
1. Bjorn Borg (SWE)
2. Jimmy Connors (USA)
3. John McEnroe (USA)
4. Vitas Gerulaitis (USA)
5. Roscoe Tanner (USA)
6. Guillermo Vilas (ARG)
7. Arthur Ashe (USA)
8. Harold Solomon (USA)
9. Jose Higueras (ESP)
10. Eddie Dibbs (USA)

1978
1. Jimmy Connors (USA)
2. Bjorn Borg (SWE)
3. Guillermo Vilas (ARG)
4. John McEnroe (USA)
5. Vitas Gerulaitis (USA)
6. Eddie Dibbs (USA)
7. Brian Gottfried (USA)
8. Raul Ramirez (MEX)
9. Harold Solomon (USA)
10. Corrado Barazzutti (ITA)

1977
1. Jimmy Connors (USA)
2. Guillermo Vilas (ARG)
3. Bjorn Borg (SWE)
4. Vitas Gerulaitis (USA)
5. Brian Gottfried (USA)
6. Eddie Dibbs (USA)
7. Manuel Orantes (ESP)
8. Raul Ramirez (MEX)
9. Ilie Nastase (ROM)
10. Dick Stockton (USA)

1976
1. Jimmy Connors (USA)
2. Bjorn Borg (SWE)
3. Ilie Nastase (ROM)
4. Manuel Orantes (ESP)
5. Raul Ramirez (MEX)
6. Guillermo Vilas (ARG)
7. Adriano Panatta (ITA)
8. Harold Solomon (USA)
9. Eddie Dibbs (USA)
10. Brian Gottfried (USA)

1975
1. Jimmy Connors (USA)
2. Guillermo Vilas (ARG)
3. Bjorn Borg (SWE)
4. Arthur Ashe (USA)
5. Manuel Orantes (ESP)
6. Ken Rosewall (AUS)
7. Ilie Nastase (ROM)
8. John Alexander (AUS)
9. Roscoe Tanner (USA)
10. Rod Laver (AUS)

1974
1. Jimmy Connors (USA)
2. John Newcombe (AUS)
3. Bjorn Borg (SWE)
4. Rod Laver (AUS)
5. Guillermo Vilas (ARG)
6. Tom Okker (NED)
7. Arthur Ashe (USA)
8. Ken Rosewall (AUS)
9. Stan Smith (USA)
10. Ilie Nastase (ROM)

1973
1. Ilie Nastase (ROM)
2. John Newcombe (AUS)
3. Jimmy Connors (USA)
4. Tom Okker (NED)
5. Stan Smith (USA)
6. Ken Rosewall (AUS)
7. Manuel Orantes (ESP)
8. Rod Laver (AUS)
9. Jan Kodes (CZE)
10. Arthur Ashe (USA)

All-Time / Singles
Open Era Title Leaders

Includes ATP World Tour, Grand Prix, WCT, Grand Slam, Grand Slam Cup. (as of May 20, 2013)

Black denotes active player

109	Jimmy Connors
94	Ivan Lendl
77	John McEnroe
76	Roger Federer
64	Bjorn Borg | Pete Sampras
62	Guillermo Vilas
60	Andre Agassi
58	Ilie Nastase
56	Rafael Nadal
49	Boris Becker | Rod Laver
44	Thomas Muster
41	Stefan Edberg
39	Stan Smith
37	Novak Djokovic
34	Michael Chang
33	Arthur Ashe | Ken Rosewall | Mats Wilander
32	John Newcombe | Manuel Orantes | Andy Roddick
31	Tom Okker
28	Lleyton Hewitt
27	Vitas Gerulaitis
26	Andy Murray | Yevgeny Kafelnikov
25	Jose-Luis Clerc | Brian Gottfried
23	Jim Courier | Yannick Noah
22	Eddie Dibbs | Goran Ivanisevic | Harold Solomon
21	Nikolay Davydenko | Andres Gomez
20	David Ferrer | Brad Gilbert | Gustavo Kuerten | Carlos Moya
19	Thomas Enqvist | Raul Ramirez
18	Marcelo Rios | Michael Stich
17	Alex Corretja | Richard Krajicek
16	Vijay Amritraj | Juan Carlos Ferrero | Roscoe Tanner | Jose Higueras

Doubles (as of May 20, 2013)

1 **Mike Bryan** / 90 - 2 **Bob Bryan** / 88 - 3 Todd Woodbridge / 83 - 4 **Daniel Nestor** / 80 - 5 Tom Okker, John McEnroe / 78 - 7 Frew McMillan / 74 - 8 Mark Woodforde / 67

9 Peter Fleming / 66 - 10 Bob Hewitt / 65 - 11 Raul Ramirez / 62 - 12 Stan Smith / 61 - 13 Marty Riessen / 60 - 14 Anders Jarryd / 58 - 15 Tomas Smid, Mark Knowles / 55

17 Jonas Bjorkman, Brian Gottfried, Paul Haarhuis, Sherwood Stewart / 54 - 21 **Mahesh Bhupathi** / 52 - 22 **Leander Paes**, Ilie Nastase / 51 - 24 Emilio Sanchez / 50

25 **Nenad Zimonjic**, Wojtek Fibak / 48 - 27 Sergio Casal / 47 - 28 **Max Mirnyi**, Rick Leach / 46 - 30 Jacco Eltingh, Bob Lutz, John Newcombe / 44

33 Martin Damm / 40 - 34 Rod Laver / 37 - 35 Patrick Galbraith / 36 - 36 Mark Edmonson / 35 - 37 Ken Flach, Kevin Ullyett / 34 - 39 Andres Gomez / 33

40 Pavel Slozil, Cyril Suk / 32 - 42 Heinz Gunthardt / 31 - 43 Roy Emerson, John Fitzgerald, David Rikl / 30 - 46 **Frantisek Cermak**, Roberto Seguso / 29

48 John Alexander, Guy Forget, Geoff Masters, Jared Palmer / 28

Black denotes active player

Emirates ATP Doubles Rankings
History of ATP World Tour No. 1

Since the introduction of the **Emirates ATP Doubles Rankings** in 1976, there have been 46 players to rank No. 1 in Doubles. Bob and Mike Bryan have ranked No. 1 for the most weeks. Here's a look at the players to rank No. 1:

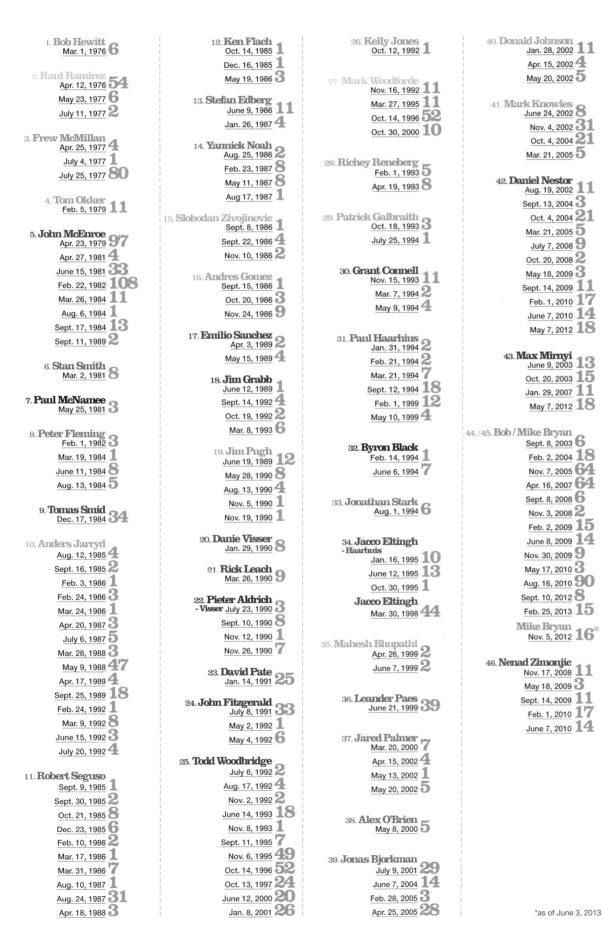

1. Bob Hewitt — Mar. 1, 1976 — 6

2. Raul Ramirez — Apr. 12, 1976 — 54 / May 23, 1977 — 6 / July 11, 1977 — 2

3. Frew McMillan — Apr. 25, 1977 — 4 / July 4, 1977 — 1 / July 25, 1977 — 80

4. Tom Okker — Feb. 5, 1979 — 11

5. John McEnroe — Apr. 23, 1979 — 97 / Apr. 27, 1981 — 4 / June 15, 1981 — 33 / Feb. 22, 1982 — 108 / Mar. 26, 1984 — 11 / Aug. 6, 1984 — 1 / Sept. 17, 1984 — 13 / Sept. 11, 1989 — 2

6. Stan Smith — Mar. 2, 1981 — 8

7. Paul McNamee — May 25, 1981 — 3

8. Peter Fleming — Feb. 1, 1982 — 3 / Mar. 19, 1984 — 1 / June 11, 1984 — 8 / Aug. 13, 1984 — 5

9. Tomas Smid — Dec. 17, 1984 — 34

10. Anders Jarryd — Aug. 12, 1985 — 4 / Sept. 16, 1985 — 2 / Feb. 3, 1986 — 1 / Feb. 24, 1986 — 3 / Mar. 24, 1986 — 1 / Apr. 20, 1987 — 3 / July 6, 1987 — 5 / Mar. 28, 1988 — 3 / May 9, 1988 — 47 / Apr. 17, 1989 — 4 / Sept. 25, 1989 — 18 / Feb. 24, 1992 — 1 / Mar. 9, 1992 — 8 / June 15, 1992 — 3 / July 20, 1992 — 4

11. Robert Seguso — Sept. 9, 1985 — 1 / Sept. 30, 1985 — 2 / Oct. 21, 1985 — 8 / Dec. 23, 1985 — 6 / Feb. 10, 1986 — 2 / Mar. 17, 1986 — 1 / Mar. 31, 1986 — 7 / Aug. 10, 1987 — 1 / Aug. 24, 1987 — 31 / Apr. 18, 1988 — 3

12. Ken Flach — Oct. 14, 1985 — 1 / Dec. 16, 1985 — 1 / May 19, 1986 — 3

13. Stefan Edberg — June 9, 1986 — 11 / Jan. 26, 1987 — 4

14. Yannick Noah — Aug. 25, 1986 — 2 / Feb. 23, 1987 — 8 / May 11, 1987 — 8 / Aug. 17, 1987 — 1

15. Slobodan Zivojinovic — Sept. 8, 1986 — 1 / Sept. 22, 1986 — 4 / Nov. 10, 1986 — 2

16. Andres Gomez — Sept. 15, 1986 — 1 / Oct. 20, 1986 — 3 / Nov. 24, 1986 — 9

17. Emilio Sanchez — Apr. 3, 1989 — 2 / May 15, 1989 — 4

18. Jim Grabb — June 12, 1989 — 1 / Sept. 14, 1992 — 4 / Oct. 19, 1992 — 2 / Mar. 8, 1993 — 6

19. Jim Pugh — June 19, 1989 — 12 / May 28, 1990 — 8 / Aug. 13, 1990 — 4 / Nov. 5, 1990 — 1 / Nov. 19, 1990 — 1

20. Danie Visser — Jan. 29, 1990 — 8

21. Rick Leach — Mar. 26, 1990 — 9

22. Pieter Aldrich - Visser — July 23, 1990 — 3 / Sept. 10, 1990 — 8 / Nov. 12, 1990 — 1 / Nov. 26, 1990 — 7

23. David Pate — Jan. 14, 1991 — 25

24. John Fitzgerald — July 8, 1991 — 33 / May 2, 1992 — 1 / May 4, 1992 — 6

25. Todd Woodbridge — July 6, 1992 — 2 / Aug. 17, 1992 — 4 / Nov. 2, 1992 — 2 / June 14, 1993 — 18 / Nov. 8, 1993 — 1 / Sept. 11, 1995 — 7 / Nov. 6, 1995 — 49 / Oct. 14, 1996 — 52 / Oct. 13, 1997 — 24 / June 12, 2000 — 20 / Jan. 8, 2001 — 26

26. Kelly Jones — Oct. 12, 1992 — 1

27. Mark Woodforde — Nov. 16, 1992 — 11 / Mar. 27, 1995 — 11 / Oct. 14, 1996 — 52 / Oct. 30, 2000 — 10

28. Richey Reneberg — Feb. 1, 1993 — 5 / Apr. 19, 1993 — 8

29. Patrick Galbraith — Oct. 18, 1993 — 3 / July 25, 1994 — 1

30. Grant Connell — Nov. 15, 1993 — 11 / Mar. 7, 1994 — 2 / May 9, 1994 — 4

31. Paul Haarhuis — Jan. 31, 1994 — 2 / Feb. 21, 1994 — 2 / Mar. 21, 1994 — 7 / Sept. 12, 1994 — 18 / Feb. 1, 1999 — 12 / May 10, 1999 — 4

32. Byron Black — Feb. 14, 1994 — 1 / June 6, 1994 — 7

33. Jonathan Stark — Aug. 1, 1994 — 6

34. Jacco Eltingh - Haarhuis — Jan. 16, 1995 — 10 / June 12, 1995 — 13 / Oct. 30, 1995 — 1 / **Jacco Eltingh** Mar. 30, 1998 — 44

35. Mahesh Bhupathi — Apr. 26, 1999 — 2 / June 7, 1999 — 2

36. Leander Paes — June 21, 1999 — 39

37. Jared Palmer — Mar. 20, 2000 — 7 / Apr. 15, 2002 — 4 / May 13, 2002 — 1 / May 20, 2002 — 5

38. Alex O'Brien — May 8, 2000 — 5

39. Jonas Bjorkman — July 9, 2001 — 29 / June 7, 2004 — 14 / Feb. 28, 2005 — 3 / Apr. 25, 2005 — 28

40. Donald Johnson — Jan. 28, 2002 — 11 / Apr. 15, 2002 — 4 / May 20, 2002 — 5

41. Mark Knowles — June 24, 2002 — 8 / Nov. 4, 2002 — 31 / Oct. 4, 2004 — 21 / Mar. 21, 2005 — 5

42. Daniel Nestor — Aug. 19, 2002 — 11 / Sept. 13, 2004 — 3 / Oct. 4, 2004 — 21 / Mar. 21, 2005 — 5 / July 7, 2008 — 9 / Oct. 20, 2008 — 2 / May 18, 2009 — 3 / Sept. 14, 2009 — 11 / Feb. 1, 2010 — 17 / June 7, 2010 — 14 / May 7, 2012 — 18

43. Max Mirnyi — June 9, 2003 — 13 / Oct. 20, 2003 — 15 / Jan. 29, 2007 — 11 / May 7, 2012 — 18

44. / 45. Bob / Mike Bryan — Sept. 8, 2003 — 6 / Feb. 2, 2004 — 18 / Nov. 7, 2005 — 64 / Apr. 16, 2007 — 64 / Sept. 8, 2008 — 6 / Nov. 3, 2008 — 2 / Feb. 2, 2009 — 15 / June 8, 2009 — 14 / Nov. 30, 2009 — 9 / May 17, 2010 — 3 / Aug. 16, 2010 — 90 / Sept. 10, 2012 — 8 / Feb. 25, 2013 — 15 / **Mike Bryan** Nov. 5, 2012 — 16*

46. Nenad Zimonjic — Nov. 17, 2008 — 11 / May 18, 2009 — 3 / Sept. 14, 2009 — 11 / Feb. 1, 2010 — 17 / June 7, 2010 — 14

as of June 3, 2013

Total Weeks at No. 1

WEEKS AT NO. 1		WEEKS AT NO. 1	
Mike Bryan (USA)	*330	Pieter Aldrich (RSA)	19
Bob Bryan (USA)	314	Yannick Noah (FRA)	19
John McEnroe (USA)	269	Grant Connell (CAN)	17
Todd Woodbridge (AUS)	205	Peter Fleming (USA)	17
Daniel Nestor (CAN)	113	Jared Palmer (USA)	17
Anders Jarryd (SWE)	107	Stefan Edberg (SWE)	15
Frew McMillan (RSA)	85	Andres Gomez (ECU)	13
Mark Woodforde (AUS)	84	Jim Grabb (USA)	13
Jonas Bjorkman (SWE)	74	Richey Reneberg (USA)	13
Paul Haarhuis (NED)	69	Tom Okker (NED)	11
Jacco Eltingh (NED)	68	Rick Leach (USA)	9
Mark Knowles (BAH)	65	Byron Black (ZIM)	8
Raul Ramirez (MEX)	62	Stan Smith (USA)	8
Robert Seguso (USA)	62	Slobodan Zivojinovic (YUG)	7
Max Mirnyi (BLR)	57	Bob Hewitt (RSA)	6
Nenad Zimonjic (SRB)	56	Emilio Sanchez (ESP)	6
John Fitzgerald (AUS)	40	Jonathan Stark (USA)	6
Leander Paes (IND)	39	Ken Flach (USA)	5
Tomas Smid (CZE)	34	Alex O'Brien (USA)	5
Danie Visser (RSA)	27	Mahesh Bhupathi (IND)	4
Jim Pugh (USA)	26	Patrick Galbraith (USA)	4
David Pate (USA)	25	Paul McNamee (AUS)	3
Donald Johnson (USA)	20	Kelly Jones (AUS)	1

*as of June 3, 2013

Year-End Doubles No. 1

2012	Mike Bryan
2011	Bob Bryan-Mike Bryan
2010	Bob Bryan-Mike Bryan
2009	Bob Bryan-Mike Bryan
2008	Nenad Zimonjic
2007	Bob Bryan-Mike Bryan
2006	Bob Bryan-Mike Bryan
2005	Bob Bryan-Mike Bryan
2004	Mark Knowles-Daniel Nestor
2003	Max Mirnyi
2002	Mark Knowles
2001	Jonas Bjorkman
2000	Mark Woodforde
1999	Leander Paes
1998	Jacco Eltingh
1997	Todd Woodbridge
1996	Todd Woodbridge-Mark Woodforde
1995	Todd Woodbridge
1994	Paul Haarhuis
1993	Grant Connell
1992	Mark Woodforde
1991	John Fitzgerald
1990	Pieter Aldrich-Danie Visser
1989	Anders Jarryd
1988	Anders Jarryd
1987	Robert Seguso
1986	Andres Gomez
1985	Robert Seguso
1984	Tomas Smid
1983	John McEnroe
1982	John McEnroe
1981	John McEnroe
1980	John McEnroe
1979	John McEnroe
1978	Frew McMillan
1977	Frew McMillan
1976	Raul Ramirez

Red denotes active player

*as of June 3, 2013

Credits & Acknowledgements

Editorial Direction
Nicola Arzani
Simon Higson

Creative Direction
George Ciz

Contributors
Peter Bodo
Neil Harman
Leo Schlink
Ed Smith

Design
Junction Design

Data and Analysis
Greg Sharko

ATP Contributors
Geoffroy Bourbon
James Buddell
Martin Dagahs
Nanette Duxin
Richard Evans
Lucy Flory
Susie Hygate
Alison Kim
Alison Lee
Paul Macpherson

Special Thanks
Russ Adams
Mike Tette
Gianni Ciaccia
Rolex, founding partner of
the ATP Heritage Programme.

Photo Credits
Images Courtesy of Getty Images
and ATP World Tour Tournaments.

Cover **Red Photographic**, **Junction Design** Inside Cover **Tom Shaw/Getty Images** P2-3 **Ryan Pierse/Getty Images**, **Red Photographic** P4-5 **Adam Pretty/Getty Images** P7 **AFP/Getty Images**, **Getty Images**, **Tony Duffy/Getty Images**, **Tony Duffy/Getty Images**, **ATP/Getty Images**, **Timothy A Clary/AFP/Getty Images** P8 **Clive Brunskill/Getty Images**, **Al Bello/Getty Images**, **Julian Finney/Getty Images** P9 **Glyn Kirk/AFP/Getty Images** P10-11 **Mark Kolbe/Getty Images** P12-13 **Russ Adams Productions** P14 **Russ Adams Productions**, **Russ Adams Productions**, **AFP/Getty Images**, **AFP/Getty Images** P15 **Russ Adams Productions**, **Mike Lawn/Getty Images**, **Russ Adams Productions** P16-17 **Russ Adams Productions** P18 **Russ Adams Productions**, **Russ Adams Productions** P19 **Russ Adams Productions**, **Tony Duffy/Getty Images**, **CBS via Getty Images**, **Tony Duffy/Getty Images**, **Tony Duffy/Getty Images** P20-21 **Getty Images** P22 **Tony Duffy/Getty Images**, **Daniel Simon/Gamma-Rapho via Getty Images**, **Michael Brennan/Getty Images**, P23 **AFP/Getty Images**, **Getty Images** P24-25 **Walter Iooss Jr./Sports Illustrated/Getty Images** P26 **Steve Powell/Getty Images**, **Getty Images**, **Tony Duffy/Getty Images**, **Tony Duffy/Getty Images** P27 **Steve Powell/Getty Images**, **Getty Images**, **Russ Adams Productions** P28 **Getty Images**, **Reg Burkett/Getty Images**, **Russ Adams Productions**, **BINH/AFP/Getty Images**, **AFP/Getty Images** P29 **Tony Duffy/Getty Images**, **Russ Adams Productions**, **Getty Images**, **Steve Powell/Getty Images** P30-31 **Chris Cole/Getty Images**, **Bob Martin/Getty Images** P32 **Russ Adams Productions**, **Steve Powell/Getty Images** P33 **Russell Cheyne/Getty Images**, **Getty Images**, **Getty Images**, **Russ Adams Productions** P34-35 **Getty Images**, **Joel Robine/AFP/Getty Images** P36 **Russ Adams Productions**, **Getty Images** P37 **Russ Adams Productions**, **Bob Martin/Getty Images**, **Russ Adams Productions** P38-39 **David Walberg/Sports Illustrated/Getty Images** P40 **Russ Adams Productions**, **Pascal Rondeau/Getty Images**, **Dan Smith/Getty Images**, **Bob Martin/Getty Images** P41 **Bob Thomas/Bob Thomas Sports Photography/Getty Images** P42-43 **Simon Bruty/Getty Images** P44 **Gary M. Prior/Getty Images**, **Russ Adams Productions**, **Bob Martin/Getty Images**, **Cynthia Lum** P45 **Derrick Ceyrac/**

AFP/Getty Images, **David Callow/AFP/Getty Images**, **Pierre Verdy/AFP Getty Images** P46 **Getty Images**, **Pierre Verdy/AFP/Getty Images**, **Russ Adams** P47 **Getty Images**, **Pascal Rondeau/Getty Images**, **Simon Bruty/Getty Images**, **Gary M. Prior/Getty Images** P48-49 **Clive Brunskill/Getty Images**, **Gary M. Prior/Getty Images**, P50 **Gary M. Prior/Getty Images**, **Joyce Naltchayan/AFP/Getty Images**, **Chris Cole/Getty Images**, **Clive Brunskill/Getty Images**, **Time Life Pictures/Getty Images**, **Clive Brunskill/Getty Images** P51 **Gianni Ciaccia/Sport Vision**, **Stan Honda/AFP/Getty Images**, **Eddi Yu/edyufoto** P52-53 **Al Bello/Getty Images**, **Stu Foster/Getty Images** P54 **Clive Brunskill/Getty Images**, **Henri Szwarc/Bongarts/Getty Images** P55 **Clive Brunskill/Getty Images**, **Clive Brunskill/Getty Images**, **Ezra Shaw/Getty Images**, **Mike Powell/Getty Images**, **Evan Agostini/Getty Images**, **Clive Brunskill/Getty Images** P56-57 **Martin Rose/Bongarts/Getty Images**, **Gianni Ciaccia/Sport Vision** P58 **Roberto Schmidt/AFP/Getty Images**, **Frank Peters/Bongarts/Getty Images**, **Stu Forster/Getty Images**, **Pascal George/AFP/Getty Images**, **Brian Bahr/Getty Images**, **Henri Szwarc/Bongarts/Getty Images** P59 **Gianni Ciaccia/Sport Vision**, **Gianni Ciaccia/Sport Vision**, **Al Bello/Getty Images**, **Gianni Ciaccia/Sport Vision**, **Scott Barbour/Getty Images** P60-61 **Nick Laham/Getty Images**, **Scott Barbour/Getty Images**, **Scott Barbour/Getty Images** P62 **Ezra Shaw/Getty Images**, **Clive Brunskill/Getty Images**, **Tony McDonough/Getty Images**, **Nick Laham/Getty Images** P63 **Mike Simons/AFP/Getty Images**, **Scott Barbour/Getty Images**, **Scott Barbour/Getty Images**, **Nick Laham/Getty Images**, **Nick Laham/Getty Images** P64-65 **Matt Campbell/AFP/Getty Images**, **Clive Brunskill/Getty Images**, **Matthew Stockman/Getty Images** P66 **Adam Pretty/Getty Images**, **Matthew Stockman/Getty Images** P67 **Sergio Perez/AFP/Getty Images**, **Timothy A Clary/AFP/Getty Images**, **Matt Campbell/AFP/Getty Images**, **Matthew Stockman/Getty Images**, **Matt Campbell/AFP/Getty Images**, **Brian Bahr/Getty Images**, **Clive Brunskill/Getty Images** P68 **Bob Martin/Getty Images**, **Mark Sandten/Bongarts/Getty Images**, **Roberto Schmidt/AFP/Getty Images**, **Hector Mata/AFP/Getty Images** P69 **Martin Rose/Bongarts/Getty Images**, **Roberto**

Schmidt/AFP/Getty Images, **Al Bello/Getty Images**, **Al Bello/Getty Images** P70-71 **Al Bello/Getty Images**, **Jasper Juinen/Getty Images**, **Daniel Berehulak/Getty Images**, **Julian Finney/Getty Images** P72 **Phil Cole/Getty Images**, **Julian Finney/Getty Images** P73 **Adam Pretty/Getty Images**, **Julian Finney/Getty Images**, **Cameron Spencer/Getty Images**, **Stuart Franklin/Bongarts/Getty Images**, **ATP World Tour**, **Max Douglas/Getty Images**, **ATP World Tour**, **Jamie McDonald/Getty Images for Laureus**, **Ryan Pierse/Getty Images for Laureus** P74-75 **Clive Brunskill/Getty Images**, **Julian Finney/Getty Images** P76 **Ryan Pierse/Getty Images**, **Ronald Martinez/Getty Images**, **Ronald Martinez/Getty Images** P77 **Alexander Hassenstein/Bongarts/Getty Images**, **Clive Brunskill/Getty Images**, **Victor Fralle/Getty Images**, **Jasper Juinen/Getty Images**, **Julian Finney/Getty Images** P78-79 **Ryan Pierse/Getty Images** P80 **Frederic J. Brown/AFP/Getty Images** P81 **Jean Christophe Magnenet/AFP/Getty Images**, **Michael Dodge/Getty Images**, **Julian Finney/Getty Images**, **Clive Brunskill/Getty Images**, **Andreas Solaro/Getty Images**, **Mark Dadswell/Getty Images**, **Julian Finney/Getty Images**, **Clive Brunskill/Getty Images**, **Clive Mason/Getty Images** P82 **William West/AFP/Getty Images**, **Julian Finney/Getty Images**, **Ryan Pierse/Getty Images** P83 **ATP World Tour**, **Chris Trotman/Getty Images**, **Andreas Solaro/AFP/Getty Images**, **AFP/Getty Images** P84-85 **Marianna Massey/Getty Images** P86 **AFP/Getty Images** P87 **Gary M. Prior/Getty Images** P88 **Gary M. Prior/Getty Images** P89 **Robert Sullivan/AFP/Getty Images** P90 **Mike Nelson/AFP/Getty Images** P91 **Carol Newsom/AFP/Getty Images** P92 **Getty Images** P93 **Adam Pretty/Getty Images** P94 **Pierre-Philippe Marcou/AFP/Getty Images** P95 **Gary M. Prior/Getty Images** P96-97 **Marianna Massey/Getty Images** P98 **AFP/Getty Images**, **Adrian Murrell/Getty Images**, **Getty Images**, **Steve Powell/Getty Images**, **Bob Martin/Getty Images**, **Joel Robine/AFP/Getty Images**, **Bob Martin/Getty Images**, **Gary M. Prior/Getty Images**, **Jacques Demarthon/AFP/Getty Images** P99 **Gary M. Prior/Getty Images**, **Stu Forster/Getty Images**, **Adam Pretty/Getty Images**, **Nick Laham/Getty Images**, **Nick Laham/Getty Images**, **Peter Parks/AFP/Getty Images**, **Vince Caligiuri/Getty Images**.